So What
Difference Does
Faith Make
in My World?

Joey O'Connor has worked in youth and family ministry for fifteen years in Southern California. He is a conference speaker and author of fourteen books for couples, parents, and young adults. He lives with his wife and four children in San Clemente, California, where he likes to surf, eat fish tacos, and lie in the hot sand.

His works include:

So What Does God Have to Do with Who I Am?

So What's the Deal with Love?

You're Grounded for Life & 49 Other Crazy Things Parents Say

Have Your Wedding Cake and Eat It Too: You Can Be Happy and Married

I Know You Love Me, But Do You Like Me? Becoming Your Mate's Best Friend

Women Are Always Right & Men Are Never Wrong

Heaven's Not a Crying Place: Teaching Your Child about Funerals, Death, & the Life Beyond

In His Steps: The Promise

Excuse Me! I'll Take My Piece of the Planet Now

Whadd'ya Gonna Do? 25 Steps for Getting a Life

Breaking Your Comfort Zones

Graffiti for Gen X Guys by J. David Schmidt with Joey O'Connor

Graffiti for Gen X Girls by J. David Schmidt with Joey O'Connor

For speaking events, conferences, and seminars, please call 1-877-447-4377. You can also write to Joey O'Connor at P.O. Box 3373, San Clemente, CA 92674-3373. Visit Joey's web site at http://www.joeyo.com. You can email Joey with your comments and questions at: joey@joeyo.com

So What
Difference Does
Faith Make
in My World?

Joey O'Connor

Fleming H. Revell
A Division of Baker Book House Co
Grand Rapids, Michigan 49516

© 2002 by Joey O'Connor

Published by Fleming H. Revell
a division of Baker Book House Company
P.O. Box 6287, Grand Rapids, MI 49516-6287

Printed in the United States of America

ISBN 0-8007-5769-6

Library of Congress Cataloging-in-Publication Data is on file at the Library of Congress, Washington, D.C.

Scripture is from the HOLY BIBLE, NEW INTERNATIONAL VERSION®. NIV®. Copyright © 1973, 1978, 1984 by International Bible Society. Used by permission of Zondervan Publishing House. All rights reserved.

For current information about all releases from Baker Book House, visit our web site:

http://www.bakerbooks.com

To Ellie Sophia O'Connor

I love your hugs.
I love your smile.
I love our little dates.
I love being your daddy.

You'll always be my little girl.

Contents

Introduction

There are a lot of things in this world that make absolutely no difference. For example, take loading the dishwasher. Your mom tells you to load the dishwasher, and like the best teenager on this planet, you do just as she asks. No whining. No complaining. No pouty attitude about missing your favorite sitcom. You do what she says. *No problema.*

You haven't so much as placed a single fork into the silverware basket when your mom suddenly says, "That's upside down! Forks are placed in the silverware basket pointy side up."

"No. No. No," you reply. "People might gouge their fingertips when they're unloading the dishwasher."

Your mom gets a curt little look on her face and says, "No. No. No. If the fork is not placed upright in the silverware basket, the dried tuna casserole scum will not come off. The fork goes in pointy side up."

You get her point, but you certainly don't agree with it. What difference does it make how silverware is loaded? It doesn't. None whatsoever. We both know that, but there's a lot of disagreement over what makes a difference and what doesn't

A big part of growing up is separating what is truly important in life and what isn't. By seeking to find those things that can make the greatest difference in your life, you can enjoy a quality of life you never imagined.

Think about it: In middle school, high school, and college, young people like you set out to find what really makes a difference in life. So, you may be into fashion and the latest clothes. One of your friends may be into sports. Another friend might be into making music. Still another might like surfing the Internet and taking computers apart. You and your friends pursue your interests and activities, because these things, in one way or another, make a difference in your lives.

On the other hand, some young people pursue things that can have a negative effect on their lives. A lot of young people experiment with drugs and alcohol or premarital sex or risky behaviors because it makes *some sort of difference* in their lives, but it's the type of difference that doesn't bring lasting satisfaction. Other young people look to popularity or good grades or success or their music or a boyfriend or girlfriend to find meaning and purpose. None of these offer ultimate satisfaction either.

By now, you're probably asking yourself, "Okay, some things make a difference in my life and other things don't; *so what difference does faith make in my world?*"

My answer is, "All the difference in the world."

All of us search for the very things that we think will make the most difference in our lives. Our heart is set on a journey, a mission if you will, to find out what will give us lasting satisfaction in this life, and we'll be restless until we discover what that one thing is. The Bible says that God has set eternity in the hearts of men. Our hearts have an eternal longing for meaning and purpose and satisfaction. The Bible also says that this longing, this deep thirst, will only be satisfied with the very God who created our hearts and who designed us to enjoy him forever.

Your faith makes all the difference in the world because as the apostle Paul says, "without faith it is impossible to please God" (Heb. 11:6a). Without faith you can't know God. You can't love God. You can't please God. Without faith you can't meet the source of all satisfaction. It is by faith that you are able to "believe that [God] exists and that he rewards those who earnestly seek him" (Heb. 11:6b).

Friend, consider this. Everyone you know seeks something or someone because there's some type of reward involved. Your faith makes a difference because God rewards those who earnestly seek him, and in seeking him, you'll discover a lasting satisfaction in your life you never could have imagined was possible.

"But where do I start?" you may ask. "I don't know much about God or Jesus or the Bible." Whether you know a lot about God and the Bible or nothing at all, the good news is that God starts right where you're at. The Bible says that faith is a gift, and faith comes through hearing the Word of God. So, here's your gift. It's God's Word written so you can know he loves you and so you can learn to love him in a way that will make an amazing difference in your life.

As you flip through the pages of this book, you'll discover that God, through his Word, has something relevant to say about every part of your life. You'll also find here all sorts of stories about how to put your faith into action and great ideas for making it through your teenage years with the One who will give your life meaning and satisfaction. Just dig in and find out what a difference faith makes. We won't argue over forks. I think you'll get the point, but I promise not to draw any blood.

School Survival School Survival
School Survival School Survival
School Survival School Survival
School Survival School Survival
School Survival School Survival
School Survival hool Survival
School Survival School Survival
School Survival School Survival
Sch School Survival urvival
School Survival School Survival

1

School Survival

Junior high and high school years weren't easy for me. In the short span of six years, I attended five different schools – two private and three public. That means I was a "new kid" five times. I hated being a new kid. The only school I didn't attend during junior high and high school was military school. I deserve a medal. Five of 'em. I'm a school survivor.

If you've hopped from school to school or if you're just trying to survive school one day at a time, then we've got a lot in common. Unlike most kids who switch schools often, my dad wasn't in the military nor did his company ship him all over the western United States. *We only moved once!* How I went to five schools in six years, I'm still trying to figure out. Here's the abbreviated version of my school survival history guide (I've left out the gory details for those of you with weak stomachs):

Fifth grade: Valentine Elementary. I was a happy, unassuming little kid. Had an idyllic life. Little did I know what lay ahead.

Sixth and seventh grade: We moved. My first private school. Fear. Weird uniforms. New kids. Made a touchdown. Made friends.

Eighth grade: Niguel Hills Junior High. New school. Big place. Got lost first day of school. Almost cried trying to find classroom. Cool year. Skateboard team. Made lots of friends. First kiss. . . . Wow!

Freshman year: Resentencing. What did I do? Another prison, er, private school. A forty-five-minute drive. Weirder uniforms. Few friends. Complained all year long. (Ask my folks.)

Sophomore year: Begged. Pleaded. Made runaway threats. Parents relented. Another new school. My choice. Parole granted upon good behavior.

Senior year: Graduation. Finally free.

Surviving school can be the toughest thing you face as a teenager. But going to school can also be a positive experience: You get to meet new friends, share memories with old ones, and do all sorts of things you never got to do before. There are clubs, sports teams, activities, and all kinds of adventures just waiting to be experienced. Some students I know absolutely love school. Others can't stand it. For those who hate it, school can be a daily slaughterhouse: They're sick of the cliques, the popularity game, the competition. They hate the pressure to use drugs and alcohol and to be sexually active. For them, school isn't an education; it's a daily punishment for something they didn't do.

Most students live somewhere between these two extremes. School has its good points; it has its bad points. If school was really that bad, anarchy would have reigned long ago. On the

School Survival

average, most students would give school a C⁺/B-. School is school. It's okay. The majority of teenagers accept school for what it is: the good, the bad, the ugly, the games, the teachers, the rules, the cafeteria food, the homework, the dating scene, the whole enchilada. School can be more than mere survival. It doesn't have to be a harsh life filled with meaningless drudgery, piles of homework, and irrelevant geometry exams.

Whatever your experience with school has been so far, God wants you to know that he cares about you; he also cares about your school. He's concerned about you every morning when you wake up and head out the door to school. He cares about your friends, your homework, the pressures you face, and the questions you have about your future. He wants to be involved in your life. When you feel swatted down, he wants to pick you up. If you're lonely after a fight with a friend, he will be your friend. This chapter is loaded with info about how God can help you be more than a survivor on your campus. In every situation or problem you encounter, he's ready to be a teacher, friend, coach, nurse, noon aide, janitor, and father who's cheering for you in the stands. Knowing God's own Son, Jesus Christ, makes life an adventure and not just another assignment. Better yet, God doesn't give homework. You're already an "A" in his book.

Being like Jesus

Ambassadors for God

What if you were sent to East Africa as a United Nations Ambassador? What if it was your responsibility to help the millions of starving people in one of its war-torn countries? Would

Not Until You've Finished Your Homework

Proven Principles for Paralyzing Procrastination

pro-cras-ti-nate: To put off, esp. habitually, doing something until a future time, like homework. A great way to grind your parents, get grounded, and get major grief from teachers and low, gruesome grades.

Fess up, admit it, you're a habitual offender. When it comes to finishing your homework, you've got a rap sheet longer than the word itself. Cut into bite-size

(There's more!)

☞

you go? In the name of God, would you have the compassion of Christ to help those who can't help themselves? Radical way to think, huh?

You don't have to go to Africa or India or South America to do something radical for Jesus. You don't have to wait for God to sky-write a message across the wild-blue yonder to tell you what to do for him. You can go right to your campus where there are students starving for friendship. Starving for attention. Hungry for love. Desperate for someone who cares. You can do something radical for God today.

If you're a Christian, you're an official representative of Jesus Christ. You are an ambassador for Jesus. You represent his love, his interests, his concern for every person who doesn't know him. The way to be an ambassador for Jesus is to make a dif-

Being like Jesus

pieces, your horrendous homework wouldn't be so bad, but *NNNOOOOO . . . you've chosen the hard way.* Like other homework hoodlums your age, you are a *PRO-CRAS-TI-NA-TOR!!!*

Perhaps as you read this pummeling indictment of your proliferating procrastinating ways, you have been banished to your bedroom to complete your three chapters in science (twenty pages each chapter, small print, questions at the end), write an English essay on the Enlightenment Period in Post-Café-Latte Europe, memorize one hundred Spanish verbs in the past-participle tense, create an authentic Daniel Boone log cabin circa 1820 complete with indigenous flora, and develop an eight-page outline of the opposing views of Einstein's theory of relativity in relationship to today's tidal changes. Here are the proven principles you need to paralyze the procrastination in your life . . . read these now . . . *don't put off for tomorrow what you can do today and was due yesterday!*

(One to go!!)

☞

ference for him one person at a time. It's crazy to think that you have to do everything. Loving other people in the name of Christ doesn't depend on you; God works *through* you. All you need to do is to be willing and available. Some people would rather get sent to Africa than take a stand for Christ in their classroom. Remember: You don't have to take on your whole campus. Just be an ambassador, a friend to someone who's starving for acceptance. With that type of love, you'll be able to feed the world.

I want to help a girl who's got a lot of problems, but how can I help her without sounding stupid?

"In everything I did, I showed you that by this kind of hard work we must help the weak, remembering the words the Lord Jesus himself

Being like Jesus

Principle #1: Cancel all cable subscriptions, Internet access accounts, and shortwave radio reception. No more ESPN or *Leave It to Beaver* reruns.

Principle #2: Call your girlfriend(s) and tell her (them) you are leaving the country for a short while. Then cut the phone line.

Principle #3: No fridge breaks, potty breaks, or do-nothing breaks.

Principle #4: *Don't even think of playing Nintendo or SEGA!*

Principle #5: Get yourself a professional agent and have him cut a major deal with your parents if you complete all your homework in a given time period.

Principle #6: Create a chair that zaps you every time you get up. (Your science teacher will probably give you extra credit for this one!)

Principle #7: Get to work.

Principle #8: Read principle #7 again!

(That's all!)

said: 'It is more blessed to give than to receive.'"

ACTS 20:35

I've talked about Christ to this guy in my P.E. class; how can I find the courage to keep talking to him?

Pray also for me, that whenever I open my mouth, words may be given me so that I will fearlessly make known the mystery of the gospel.

EPHESIANS 6:19

I want to be a witness for Jesus on my campus; what does God want to say through my life?

We are therefore Christ's ambassadors, as though God were making his appeal through us. We implore you on Christ's behalf: Be reconciled to God.

2 CORINTHIANS 5:20

How can I be the person Jesus wants me to be?

"You are the light of the world. A city on a hill cannot be hidden. Neither do people light a lamp and put it under a bowl. Instead they put it on its stand, and it gives light to everyone in the house. In the same way, let your light shine before men, that they may see your good deeds and praise your Father in heaven."

MATTHEW 5:14–16

Being like Jesus

Should I be concerned about what others think of me as a Christian?

I am not ashamed of the gospel, because it is the power of God for the salvation of everyone who believes: first for the Jew, then for the Gentile.

ROMANS 1:16

How can God help me remain faithful to him?

That is why I am suffering as I am. Yet I am not ashamed, because I know whom I have believed, and am convinced that he is able to guard what I have entrusted to him for that day.

2 TIMOTHY 1:12

My friends always pick on this little freshman guy; what should I do?

Defend the cause of the weak and fatherless; maintain the rights of the poor and oppressed. Rescue the weak and needy; deliver them from the hand of the wicked.

PSALM 82:3–4

Should I try to get to know the unpopular people at my school?

Better to be lowly in spirit and among the oppressed than to share plunder with the proud.

PROVERBS 16:19

How does God want me to make a difference on my campus?

"The Spirit of the Lord is on me, because he has anointed me to preach good news to the poor. He has sent me to proclaim freedom for the prisoners and recovery of sight for the blind, to release the oppressed."

LUKE 4:18

Being like Jesus

Changing Your World

Be a Difference-Maker

 Want a simple way to be a difference-maker? Here's a great idea that worked for us. It may work for you. Our youth ministry needed money to help students go on trips. At the same time, we wanted to serve our community by doing the dirty work no one else wanted to do. A friend of mine in the Midwest told me how to raise money and serve the community at the same time. It sounded like a good idea, so we went for it.

Like any other work-a-thon, students raised money from family and friends for a one-day work project we called Project Serve. Instead of going surfing, to the mall, mountain bike riding, or to the gym, about fifty students set out in teams to work their tails off for a whole day. One group cut a nature trail. Another group yanked weeds in a dirt lot the size of two football fields. Other teams painted a YMCA, planted flowers, and

Breaking Your Comfort Zones

Garbage dumps. Gross smells. Broken glass. Dogs that look like walking roadkills. Runny noses and dirty faces. Children playing in a graveyard. I don't know about you, but poverty and starvation gross me out. And whenever something grosses me out, I try to forget about it. Yesterday I got grossed out,

(Read on!!)
☞

but I'm not trying to forget about what I experienced. I'd be a fool if I did.

Six friends of mine and I drove down from our nice, comfortable homes and lifestyles in Orange County, California (home of every creature comfort imaginable: Dizzyland, Knott's Scary Farm, Tragic Mountain, The Beaches, The Mountains, The Malls, etc., ad nauseam), to Tijuana, Mexico. Unlike Southern California, Tijuana seems like a place created for misery. Squatter camps filled with cardboard shacks. Open sewer trenches in the streets. Dogs you don't want to pet. There's a lot more to Tijuana than the typical tourist attractions like buying panchos, blankets, and firecrackers. Tijuana is not a comfortable place to live. Filled with poverty and despair, it's not very comfortable for your conscience. Going there sure got me out of my comfort zone.

(Turn the page!!)

☞

picked up trash in local parks. Instead of expecting to be served all the time, these students learned to make a difference through serving. You can make a difference on your campus for God. It doesn't take much effort. All you need is a willing heart and a desire to be different. It also helps to have a few friends who want to be difference makers too. Sit down and brainstorm ideas. What could you do that no one else has ever thought of? Maybe putting your garbage in the trash can is a good place to start?

My Christian friends and I want to stand out on our campus for Christ; how can we do that?

"All men will know that you are my disciples if you love one another."

JOHN 13:35

So many people at school try to bring attention to themselves; how can I be different from them?

"Not so with you. Instead, whoever wants to become great among you must be your servant, and whoever wants to be

We visited three sections of Tijuana: a poor barrio (neighborhood), the garbage dump, and an orphanage. At the barrio, we played games with kids, gave 'em showers with portable showers and tubs, helped 'em into a new set of clothes, and passed out food. The dump was pathetic. We observed hundreds of people living in tiny cardboard and plywood shacks; they scrounge for food after huge dump trucks spill tons of Tijuana garbage. We saw children in bare feet walking over endless paths of broken glass. At the orphanage, we saw more than thirty rambunctious children, their laughter replacing the horrors of life before they came to the orphanage: abuse; prostitution; poverty; abandonment.

As we moved from the barrio to the dump to the orphanage, I discovered God moving my heart from being grossed out to understanding his grace. How did it happen that you and I were born in America instead of a Tijuana barrio? How did you and I come to be the receivers of McDonald's, 429 satellite TV channels, Pizza Hut, cool clothing, BMX bikes, roller blades, and killer vacations paid for by Mom and Dad? How can we be surrounded by so many creature comforts when the rest of the world digs through garbage dumps for dinner? How can we keep from taking God's grace for granted?

(Don't stop now!!)
☞

first must be your slave—just as the Son of Man did not come to be served, but to serve, and to give his life as a ransom for many."

MATTHEW 20:26–28

How can I be like Christ among my friends?

"The greatest among you will be your servant. For whoever exalts himself will be humbled, and whoever humbles himself will be exalted."

MATTHEW 23:11–12

How can I be completely open to God's will for my life?

"I am the Lord's servant," Mary answered. "May it be to me as you have said."

LUKE 1:38

I'm a leader on my campus, but how can I be a servant too?

"Whoever serves me must follow me; and where I am, my servant also will be. My Father will honor the one who serves me."

JOHN 12:26

Does Jesus consider me his friend?

"I no longer call you servants, because a servant does not know his master's business. Instead, I have called you friends, for everything that I learned from my Father I have made known to you."

JOHN 15:15

At school, how can I demonstrate that my attitude is different?

Your attitude should be the same as that of Christ Jesus: Who, being in very nature God, did not consider equality with God something to be grasped, but made himself nothing, taking the very nature of a servant, being made in human likeness.

PHILIPPIANS 2:5–7

How can I pray for my Christian friends at school?

And we pray this in order that you may live a life worthy of the Lord and may please him in every way: bearing fruit in every good work, growing in the knowledge of God.

COLOSSIANS 1:10

The quickest but hardest way to show gratitude to God is by breaking your comfort zone. A comfort zone is that invisible, safe little circle where you don't want to be bothered by anything or anyone. It's a selfish, protective cocoon that keeps you from being who God has designed you to be. Comfort zones are great for vegging, zoning out, trading muscle for fat and turning into a spiritual Jabba the Hutt. But comfort zones are like a choke hold on your heart for spiritual growth.

Okay, so you're ready to break your comfort zone for God, but where do you start? Jesus gives some great ideas in Matthew 25: Feed the hungry; be a friend to the lonely; clothe the naked; take care of the sick; visit people in prison. Breaking your comfort zone means serving instead of zoning out. Jesus said, "Whatever you did for one of the least of these brothers of mine, you did for me." Is your little brother hungry? Make him lunch. Is there a geek in your math class no one likes? Be his friend. Are there homeless people in your town? Give them blankets. Do you know someone who's sick? Get on the phone and ask how you can help. Serving doesn't take much creativity, intelligence, or brute muscle, but it does take a lot of heart. If you're feeling "blah"

(One to go!!)

☞

Changing Your World

Cheating

Hurting Yourself

Most cheaters think they're smart. They think they know how to beat the system. When I was in eighth grade, I thought I was a smart cheater. Wrong. If you're going to cheat, you need to remember three things: (1) Never, I mean never, write down your Spanish vocabulary words on your hand; (2) never cup your hand in front of your paper, stare at it, and then write the answer on your paper; (3) never turn in your test with the same hand that has the answers on it. (I know what you're wondering: "Is this guy lame or what?")

When the test was over, my teacher asked me to stay after class. Busted! She didn't have to say much. She had me. The evidence was written all over my face. And my hand. Did I learn my lesson? No. I kept cheating for the next couple years until I finally slapped myself upside the head and asked myself, "What am I doing? What am I gaining by doing this? I may be getting a better grade, but I've also got this hollow, empty feeling inside."

You've heard it before: Cheaters never prosper. The only person you're cheating is yourself. Until you figure that out for yourself, you'll never understand. What more can I say? Don't write answers on your hand?

with God or you're just kicking back in the Jacuzzi of your comfort zone, serving others will zap that zone away. Remember: Whenever you serve others, you're serving Jesus in disguise.

Breaking your comfort zone isn't easy, but it isn't meant to be done alone. It's you and God. Cooperating together. Sledgehammer in hand. Breaking down the invisible through serving the visible. (If you're looking for 49 extremely radical ways to live for God, read Joey's book, *Breaking Your Comfort Zones*.)

(That's all!)

What should I do when the only way I'll pass this class is if I cheat?

The man of integrity walks securely, but he who takes crooked paths will be found out.

PROVERBS 10:9

The guy next to me tries to cheat off my tests; what should I do?

Be still before the LORD and wait patiently for him; do not fret when men succeed in their ways, when they carry out their wicked schemes.

PSALM 37:7

I keep telling my friend that he's going to get nailed for cheating; how can I get him to listen to me?

A man of perverse heart does not prosper; he whose tongue is deceitful falls into trouble.

PROVERBS 17:20

What harm is there in cheating?

"Whoever would love life and see good days must keep his tongue from evil and his lips from deceitful speech."

1 PETER 3:10

What can I do to avoid the temptation of cheating?

LORD, who may dwell in your sanctuary? Who may live on your holy hill? He whose walk is blameless and who does what is righteous, who speaks the truth from his heart.

PSALM 15:1–2

My friend asked me to help him cheat; I don't want to help him, but how can I tell him?

"These are the things you are to do: Speak the truth to each other."

ZECHARIAH 8:16

Cheating

What should I do when I get made fun of because I won't help others cheat on tests?

"Hear me, you who know what is right, you people who have my law in your hearts: Do not fear the reproach of men or be terrified by their insults."

ISAIAH 51:7

Doing unto Others

This One's Tough

 Mark graduated from our high school ministry a few years ago. He doesn't know it, but I used to brag about him all the time. People would ask about the ministry, and I'd tell 'em about Mark. Talking about numbers, plans, and events gets old. Talking about people like Mark makes life exciting. When I asked Mark what he did during lunch at school, he told me that two or three times a week he would look for someone having lunch by themselves. He would go up to the person sitting alone and ask if he could join them. I remember him telling me how he had lunch with a boy who had just moved into the area. Another time he had lunch with a girl who had no friends. I wish I knew ten students who had the guts to do what Mark did. Ten students who want to turn their world upside down for God. In God's eyes, Mark has class. Pure class.

Being a friend to the friendless isn't easy. Mark said that his conversations weren't always smooth. People wondered why he wanted to sit down and eat lunch with them. It wasn't as if he didn't have plenty of friends; he was just doing what God had prompted him to do. He wanted to show people that he really cared about them and that God's love had changed him in a very concrete way. Mark didn't do anything spectacular in God's eyes. He wasn't on any higher spiritual plane than you or I. As

Doing unto Others

Nobody but a Wet Baby Likes Change

When you were a baby,
you loved change. Wet to dry. Starving to
full. Bubbles to burps. Change came easy. If you
made a mess of yourself, nobody expected you to do the
dirty work. You already did your part.

Growing up, you were instrumental in helping others understand
what change was all about. Crayola-covered walls. Fashion haircuts for
the family dog. Baseballs and broken windows. Come to think of it, why
were others so resistant to change? Is it your fault your little brother didn't
understand you had become The Terminator *before* you rearranged his face? Or
why was your sister so upset her favorite doll was given an autopsy when it was
done in the name of science? When you were a kid, for the most part, change was
harder on other people than it was on you.

Now that you're a teenager, it seems that everybody is wanting you to change. Your
parents, teachers, and coaches may be sticking their mouths down your throat asking,
demanding, threatening, and pleading with you to change a negative attitude, get rid of
your spiked, multicolored hair, act more like the geek next door, or become a responsible
model citizen. But who actually takes the time to help you know what real and lasting
change is all about? Enforced changes are temporary changes. Who wants to live in an
atmosphere that is just short of a concentration camp? However, inner changes because
you choose to change are the ones that make a difference. Inner changes can last a lifetime. When you decide to make changes on the inside, you change *who* you are, not
what you are.

There's only one BIG problem: Most people are into outer changes. It's a lot easier to slip on the latest pump-up, slam-dunk, high-priced sneakers than to work
on the foul mouth you have trouble controlling. Outer change is easy. Inner
change takes work. When you make inner changes, the type that have to
do with values and personal character, you don't "kind of" change.
You either choose to make the changes or you don't. This meta-
morphosis of making personal changes is a process, an
adventure, and a journey. A transformation or modi-
fication of the real you, if you will. But before
you freak out on how much work
this is gonna take,

(Keep going!!)

☞

far as I know, he hasn't won a Nobel prize yet. Mark simply did what Jesus asks of each one of us: "Do to others."

How does Jesus want me to treat people at school?

"In everything, do to others what you would have them do to you, for this sums up the Law and the Prophets."

MATTHEW 7:12

I have some friends who are easily intimidated by other students; how can I help them?

And we urge you, brothers, warn those who are idle, encourage the timid, help the weak, be patient with everyone.

1 THESSALONIANS 5:14

How can I be more consistent in making good decisions at school?

"Simply let your 'Yes' be 'Yes,' and your 'No,' 'No.'"

MATTHEW 5:37

My friends at school are pretty skeptical about Christianity; what can I do to show them my faith is real?

Now that you have purified yourselves by obeying the truth so that you have sincere love for your brothers, love one another deeply, from the heart.

1 PETER 1:22

How can I show people at school what God's love is?

This is how we know what love is: Jesus Christ laid down his life for us. And we ought to lay down our lives for our brothers.

1 JOHN 3:16

Doing unto Others

*At my school everybody just hangs out in their own little groups;
how can we change this?*

Accept one another, then, just as Christ accepted you, in
order to bring praise to God.

ROMANS 15:7

*How can I share my faith in Christ with people at school without
turning them off?*

But in your hearts set apart Christ as Lord. Always be prepared to give an answer to everyone who asks you to give the
reason for the hope that you have. But do this with gentleness and respect.

1 PETER 3:15–16A

Is it possible for me to "live up to my reputation" as a Christian?

Let us not become weary in doing good, for at the proper
time we will reap a harvest if we do not give up.

GALATIANS 6:9

remember that it's not you who's making the changes . . . it's God!

The God who created you is the God who never changes but who is always making changes. He wants to make changes in your life that will last. He knows that real change takes time and a lot of hard work. In fact, he sent his Son, Jesus, to help you make changes you can't accomplish on your own power.

Jesus Christ, God's Son, was interested in outer changes last and inner changes first.

He faced tremendous opposition from a crowd of people who appeared perfect on the outside but who smelled like rotten meat on the inside. Jesus ripped apart the temple at First Jerusalem Savings and Loan because some people who looked good and religious on the outside were making fast cash on the local tourist trade. He refused to allow his Father's house to be changed into another ATM machine. Just as he wanted those people to change, Jesus wants you to make changes that count. Real, inner changes like honesty, purity, love, encouragement, and serving others before yourself.

If you've got some change to spare, invest it in the Creator who can transform

(Turn the page!!)

☞

Counting the Cost

Gang-Banging on Campus

"He who is not with me is against me." If you're in a gang or you have friends who are, that's the type of language you understand. You're either in the gang or not. There's no halfway, in between, or fifty-fifty. It's all or nothing. You can't live for Jesus and be in a gang; Jesus asks for total commitment. Just as a gang asks for your complete allegiance, Jesus is asking you to be totally sold out for him.

Peter, Jesus' disciple, thought that his gang could take on the Roman gang who came to take Jesus away. Peter sliced off a defenseless slave's ear with an industrial-size switchblade. Jesus told him to put the knife back in his pocket. Jesus wasn't into gang-banging; he wanted a brotherhood of peace.

If you're in a gang and have made a commitment to Christ, you need to make a decision. You may face some severe consequences for trying to get out of your gang. That's a heavy price to pay for joining a gang. You may wind up dead or beaten to a pulp for walking away. If that's the case, who do you want to end up dead for? Yourself or God? If you choose to stay in your gang, you could get nailed in the next drive-by or jumped when you least expect it. Who wins then? You're better off dead for God than dead for yourself. If you're thinking about joining a gang, slow down and think again. Joining a gang may

the impossible to the possible in your life. From spit and mud to colors and vision, the Healer made a blind man see. From falling, decaying flesh to whole, functioning limbs, the Son of God healed a leper. From a lonely and gruesome death on a cross to a bursting explosion of life for everyone, Jesus brings you and me from death to life. And that's a change you can count on.

(That's all!)

get you all sorts of things you can't get on your own: protection, money, girls, prestige, drugs, friendship, power. But what's the cost going to be? Jesus said, "What good is it for a man to gain the whole world, yet forfeit his soul? Or what can a man give in exchange for his soul? If anyone is ashamed of me and my words in this adulterous and sinful generation, the Son of Man will be ashamed of him when he comes in his Father's glory with the holy angels" (Mark 8:36 38). That's a high cost. The cost is even higher if you ignore his words.

Will God help me stop gang violence on my campus?

"Blessed are the peacemakers, for they will be called sons of God."

MATTHEW 5:9

I'm trying to tell the gang-bangers in my school to make peace, but where do I start?

Finally, all of you, live in harmony with one another; be sympathetic, love as brothers, be compassionate and humble. Do not repay evil with evil or insult with insult, but with blessing, because to this you were called so that you may inherit a blessing.

1 PETER 3:8–9

I've got a friend at school who's trying to get out of his gang, but he's afraid to do it; how can I help him?

He must turn from evil and do good; he must seek peace and pursue it.

1 PETER 3:11

I left my gang a few years ago, and I think God's calling me to help others get out; where do I begin?

"Now that I, your Lord and Teacher, have washed your feet, you also should wash one another's feet. I have set you an example that you should do as I have done for you."

JOHN 13:14–15

There's a rumor that I'm going to get jumped by some gang-bangers because I'm outspoken for Jesus; what should I do?

"Blessed are those who are persecuted because of righteousness, for theirs is the kingdom of heaven."

MATTHEW 5:10

Can I be a peacemaker on my campus?

If it is possible, as far as it depends on you, live at peace with everyone.

ROMANS 12:18

What should I do when this group of girls taunts me because I won't join their gang?

"Blessed are you when people insult you, persecute you and falsely say all kinds of evil against you because of me. Rejoice and be glad, because great is your reward in heaven, for in the same way they persecuted the prophets who were before you."

MATTHEW 5:11–12

I want to get out of my gang, but I'm afraid to take a stand for Jesus; which way should I go?

"If anyone is ashamed of me and my words, the Son of Man will be ashamed of him when he comes in his glory and in the glory of the Father and of the holy angels."

LUKE 9:26

Counting the Cost

Following Jesus

Friendship with God

Jesus hung out with a group of twelve guys a couple thousand years ago. But who does he hang out with now? If Jesus was sitting in the cafeteria at your school, would you have lunch with him? If he was a new kid on campus who just moved from Alaska, would you invite him to hang out with your friends? What if he was the last one to be picked when choosing sides for basketball? Would you pick him? A skinny, poor carpenter's son from out of town? Jesus used to have a group of buddies, but now he's looking for a new set of friends. It doesn't matter if you're a guy or a girl.

Jesus doesn't want to be left behind in church. A lot of people are good about hanging out with Jesus on Sunday, but when school rolls around Monday morning, they drop him to hang out with other friends. What do you do? Jesus wants to hang out with you every day. At school. At practice. In the library. At work. And at home. Jesus doesn't want a part-time friendship with you. He wants to go where you go and do what you do. We hear a lot of talk about following Jesus, but in reality, he follows us a lot more than we follow him. Maybe you could change something about that?

Does hanging out with Jesus mean I might lose some friends?

Then he said to them all: "If anyone would come after me, he must deny himself and take up his cross daily and follow me."

LUKE 9:23

How did Jesus have time for his Father in the midst of his busy schedule?

Following Jesus   33

Very early in the morning, while it was still dark, Jesus got up, left the house and went off to a solitary place, where he prayed.

MARK 1:35

How can I get to know Jesus better if I'm always with people?

After he had dismissed them, he went up on a mountainside by himself to pray.

MATTHEW 14:23A

I want my friends at school to know I'm a Christian, but I'm an easy target for temptation; what can I do?

"Watch and pray so that you will not fall into temptation. The spirit is willing, but the body is weak."

MATTHEW 26:41

I get torn between spending time with Jesus and spending time with my friends; what would Jesus say?

"I am the vine; you are the branches. If a man remains in me and I in him, he will bear much fruit; apart from me you can do nothing."

JOHN 15:5

How can I keep a good friendship with God?

"As the Father has loved me, so have I loved you. Now remain in my love."

JOHN 15:9

It seems so easy to get swayed away from Christ; how can I stand firm?

"If you obey my commands, you will remain in my love, just as I have obeyed my Father's commands and remain in his love."

JOHN 15:10

Following Jesus

How can I tell my friends about my relationship with Jesus?

"Come, follow me," Jesus said, "and I will make you fishers of men."

MATTHEW 4:19

Living Counterclockwise

Thoughts and Attitudes

Turn the dial counterclockwise two spins to 17, clockwise one whole spin to 34, then back again to 7 or was it 5 or 25? I always hated getting new locker combinations. At my school, they passed out

Living Your Life Backwards

Picture yourself surrounded by tombstones in the dark of a cold, windy night. Whisping billows of twisting leaves scrape and scratch across the gray-flecked monuments that mark the spot of deceased strangers. As you cautiously pass each grave site, you recognize some familiar names on a particular group of tombstones. The bitter wind stings your face, and you are shocked to discover your family plot. There! Next to Mom and Dad's grave lies your older brother who died three years ago at the age of seventy-two. And there is your younger sister's grave. She was only thirty-three! "What's going on here?" you say to yourself as part wonder, part fear races through your searching mind.

You look down and see a brown wooden cane grasped by a worn, wrinkled hand

(Don't be scared!!)

☞

locker combinations on a tiny piece of paper the size of a movie ticket, expected you to memorize the numbers before noon and then swallow the paper like a spy. Spinning the locker dial back and forth in frustration, I looked real intelligent standing in the hallway after the late bell rang. Smooth, real smooth.

Forgetting locker combinations and forgetting who we are in Christ are easy to do. Each day we get bombarded with endless messages; advertising, pressures, and television tell us how we're supposed to live our lives. The world tells us to live clockwise, yet God's message to us is completely different. He tells us to live counterclockwise. Like a locker, our minds are meant to hold all sorts of information. The right kind of information. The Bible tells us to fill our minds with his Word so we won't be swayed back and forth by every new trend that comes our way. God wants us to remember who we are in Christ. Just like we sometimes forget our locker combo, we forget about God and fill our minds with negative thoughts, comparisons, and judgments instead.

God wants to transform the way you think about him, yourself, and others. He wants you to be changed from the inside out. As you spend time getting to know God

... your hand! Your slow step is a shuffle. Your arthritic bones ache from the chilling cold. You pause to rest. You're old. Tired. Worried. Anxious. And scared. Not watching your step, you trip over a shovel lying next to a freshly dug grave. Almost falling into the six-foot-deep pit, you stumble onto a small pile of dirt and sod, only to glance down and discover a new, polished tombstone staring up at you with this menacing reminder:

**You're Next
1985–?**

Living on the Tombstone's Edge

My dad is a funeral director. An undertaker. A glorified grave digger. Even though my dad never brought home his work, when I was in junior high and high school, I saw a lot of dead bodies. You could say that motivated me to work at staying alive.

I'll never forget the time when I was at my dad's mortuary and was asked to wheel the pink casket of a dead sixteen-year-old girl to the chapel. Alone, I pushed a cold metal casket containing the lifeless body of a young girl. Just a few days earlier, she was a living, walking, talking, smiling, laughing human being. She could have been my sister. Or my girlfriend. Or the girl I sat next to in history. At that moment, that's exactly what her life was ... history.

(Keep going!!)

☞

Living Counterclockwise

better through his Word, he will transform your mind and make you the person he wants you to be. Storing his Word in your heart and mind, you'll be more inclined to remember who you are in Christ. And less inclined to forget your locker combo. Maybe.

Is it possible for me to get my mind under God's control?

The mind of sinful man is death, but the mind controlled by the Spirit is life and peace; the sinful mind is hostile to God. It does not submit to God's law, nor can it do so.

ROMANS 8:6–7

How can I put the bombardment of pressures, worries, and negative thoughts in perspective?

Finally, brothers, whatever is true, whatever is noble, whatever is right, whatever is pure, whatever is lovely, whatever is admirable—if anything is excellent or praiseworthy—think about such things.

PHILIPPIANS 4:8

How can I keep from getting so caught up in society's values that I have a hard time understanding what's important to God?

Do not conform any longer to the pattern of this world, but be transformed by the renewing of your mind. Then you will be able to test and approve what God's will is—his good, pleasing and perfect will.

ROMANS 12:2

A couple of my Christian friends disagree with me on some important issues. How can we keep these from getting in the way of our friendship?

Therefore let us stop passing judgment on one another. Instead, make up your mind not to put any stumbling block or obstacle in your brother's way.

ROMANS 14:13

As I spend time with teenagers, I occasionally ask them, "What will your tombstone say? When your life is over, what will others say about your life? When you're old and you look back on your life, what do you want to see?"

How to Live Life Backwards

The Bible says that every person will stand before God to give an account for his or her life. Jesus told his followers that death was not an option but an inevitable reality for every single person on earth. In Jesus' words, the best way to prepare for death is to prepare for eternal life through accepting his sacrificial death on a cross for your sins . . . *AND* live according to his design for your life. In Jesus Christ, you can live by dying to yourself and living for God.

(One to go!!)

☞

My friends tell me I get too cocky at times. How can I develop a better perspective on who I really am?

For by the grace given me I say to every one of you: Do not think of yourself more highly than you ought, but rather think of yourself with sober judgment, in accordance with the measure of faith God has given you.

ROMANS 12:3

My school is filled with beautiful girls; how can I keep from struggling with lust?

Rather, clothe yourselves with the Lord Jesus Christ, and do not think about how to gratify the desires of the sinful nature.

ROMANS 13:14

I've been doing really well lately by not giving into impure thoughts, but how can I keep my mind on track?

So, if you think you are standing firm, be careful that you don't fall!

1 CORINTHIANS 10:12

Developing Good Study Habits

Learn to Study

Tackle it. TV or trigonometry? Monday Night Football or music theory? Gym or geometry? Prepare for finals or procrastinate? Lousy study habits are a lot more than procrastination. They're a way of life.

So how can you develop good study habits? By applying discipline and planning to your schedule so you can *begin* to study. You have to make a decision about what you need to do: Are you going to watch TV or do algebra? Can you do both at the same time? Maybe. Maybe not. Are you going to talk on the phone or study vocab? Developing good study habits means learning how to say no so you can get the important stuff done first. That doesn't mean you can't go shoot hoops or meet your friends for a Coke. It just means you'll wait until later.

If you're a lousy student or a hopeless procrastinator, don't be too hard on yourself. If you're too hard on yourself, chances are you'll just put off your homework even more. Start where you are. Do what you can do now. If you need help, ask someone. God understands your situation. No matter what, he won't delay helping you.

My parents always get on my case for not studying enough; why should I listen to them?

The fear of the LORD is the beginning of knowledge, but fools despise wisdom and discipline.

PROVERBS 1:7

What does it take? First, live your life forward by looking at it backwards. By the time you're seventy, what would you like your relationship with God to be like? Will you have been faithful to God? Will you have forgotten him? What will you have accomplished for God? Or for yourself? What will your most important relationships look like? Whom will you have significantly influenced for God's kingdom during your life? Will the temptations, struggles, and doubts you struggle with now as a teenager have brought you closer to God or pushed him away? Will others say that you "fought the good fight, finished the race, and kept the faith" (2 Tim. 4:7)?

Jesus promises to be the author and perfecter of your faith. He promises to finish what he started. He promises to guard what he's given you. He promises to never leave or forsake you. Jesus will give you a way out when you're tempted because he is faithful. Do you want to look back on your life with a sigh of relief or a sigh of regret? Living your life backwards is the first step to living your life forward with Jesus today.

(That's all!)

Why is it that whenever my friends and I get together to study, we never get anything done?

He who heeds discipline shows the way to life, but whoever ignores correction leads others astray.

PROVERBS 10:17

I need a tutor, but why should I let someone else tell me how to do things?

Whoever loves discipline loves knowledge, but he who hates correction is stupid.

PROVERBS 12:1

I never study, and I make fun of others who do; is this sinful?

If you are wise, your wisdom will reward you; if you are a mocker, you alone will suffer.

PROVERBS 9:12

I'm trying really hard to do better in geometry, but I get easily discouraged. Can God help me?

If any of you lacks wisdom, he should ask God, who gives generously to all without finding fault, and it will be given to him.

JAMES 1:5

My classes are so frustrating, I feel like crying. Does God hear my prayers for help?

Listen to my cry for help, my King and my God, for to you I pray.

PSALM 5:2

Developing Good Study Habits

***I've blown off a lot of homework; will God help me finish it all
tonight?***

Surely God is my help; the Lord is the one who sustains me.

PSALM 54:4

Talking in Class

Quiet, Please

 Some people prove how much they don't
know by opening their mouths. Others show
how much they do know by keeping their
mouths shut. The classroom is a common proving
ground for wisdom and ignorance. When teachers
are trying to open their mouths, you can help them by shut-
ting yours. The Book of Proverbs tells us how to show our wisdom by things we say or don't say. Proverbs 25:11 says, "A
word aptly spoken is like apples of gold in settings of silver."
If you want to make a difference in your classroom, learn to
open your mouth at the right time. You don't have to be like
the people sitting next to you. Gossip kills. Lies separate close
friends. Crude remarks repel others. Cut-downs shred hearts.
Talking in class shows disrespect and a flippant attitude toward
the teacher. What if Jesus was teaching class? Would that
change what you say? What if you were teaching? How would
you like to be treated?

I get disappointed when I hear Christian students ripping on
their teachers. How can Christians praise God and curse people
made in his own image? The Book of James talks about the
power of the tongue and its destructive nature. Teachers are
people with problems, feelings, struggles, and pressures just like
you. Lighten up on 'em! Let your actions and words in class
reveal WHO you know and not just what you know. Next time
you're tempted to open your mouth with nothing to say, remem-

ber this: *En boca cerrada, no entran las moscas.* Flies don't enter a closed mouth.

This girl who sits next to me gossips all the time; what can I do?

A gossip betrays a confidence; so avoid a man who talks too much.

PROVERBS 20:19

What's wrong with a little gossip?

Whoever spreads slander is a fool.

PROVERBS 10:18

My teacher tells me that talking in class is hurting my grades. How can I change when talking is one of the best things I do?

Wise men store up knowledge, but the mouth of a fool invites ruin.

PROVERBS 10:14

My teacher always singles me out for talking; what should I do?

When words are many, sin is not absent, but he who holds his tongue is wise.

PROVERBS 10:19

There's this guy in my class who's really crude; I want to tell him to keep still, but what should I say?

The lips of the righteous know what is fitting, but the mouth of the wicked only what is perverse.

PROVERBS 10:32

I know I'm not setting a very good example as a Christian when I talk in class, but is there anything really wrong with it?

Talking in Class

Anyone, then, who knows the good he ought to do and doesn't do it, sins.

JAMES 4:17

My teacher treats us like slaves; how am I supposed to listen to someone I don't respect?

Slaves, obey your earthly masters with respect and fear, and with sincerity of heart, just as you would obey Christ.

EPHESIANS 6:5

Questioning Authority
Authority Figures

 Don't tell me! Let me guess . . . your vice-principal is a slimy, bald-headed power freak? Am I close? Let me try another: Your coach is into pain and power and takes pleasure in seeing young people bleed. Right? I thought so! Your parents? Controlling, paranoid life forms wearing polyester? Did I hit the mark? Every adult or old person over twenty-two years old is out to get you. You can't figure out what you've done, but you know they're against you, right? That's why you question authority? I thought so.

One of the teens in our youth ministry had a real problem with authority. In his eyes, every coach, teacher, and boss was out to nail him. This guy never seemed to understand that the world didn't revolve around him. If things didn't go his way, it was always someone else's fault. *The coach hates me. This teacher's always picking on me. My boss never gives me weekends off.* Excuses. One after another. At times, his excuses and justifications drove me so crazy, I felt like screaming in his face, "What's the matter with you? Open your eyes. The problem isn't them. It's you!"

Questioning authority is okay if you're searching for truth. Questioning authority is okay if there's a clear abuse of authority. But questioning or challenging authority so you can get your own way is selfish. It's called manipulation. Trying to get your own way by blaming your problems on others is like spitting in the wind. Many students have problems with authority because of poor relationships with their parents. For someone who's been beaten or sexually abused by an older person, it makes perfect sense they're not going to trust anyone. For an abused person, questioning authority is a means for protection and self-preservation. That's healthy. Questioning authority in order to avoid responsibility or to blame others doesn't count. If you can't accept authority from others, how will you ever learn to accept God's authority in your life? Question authority for truth's sake, not your own.

It seems that every adult at my school wants to order me around; what can I do?

Submit yourselves for the Lord's sake to every authority instituted among men.

1 PETER 2:13A

I can't understand why our school has the worst principal in the world; how did God let that happen?

Everyone must submit himself to the governing authorities, for there is no authority except that which God has established. The authorities that exist have been established by God.

ROMANS 13:1

Is it okay to rebel against school rules that everyone thinks are wrong anyway?

Consequently, he who rebels against the authority is rebelling against what God has instituted, and those who do so will bring judgment on themselves.

ROMANS 13:2

Does God expect me to respect a vice-principal who's completely unrespectable?

Give everyone what you owe him . . . if respect, then respect; if honor, then honor.

ROMANS 13:7

I know it's right to listen to school authorities, but there's something inside me that can't wait to rebel; what should I do?

Submit yourselves, then, to God. Resist the devil, and he will flee from you.

JAMES 4:7

My friends and I have a really hard time dealing with authority; whom should I listen to?

Blessed is the man who does not walk in the counsel of the wicked or stand in the way of sinners or sit in the seat of mockers.

PSALM 1:1

I don't want to cause trouble at school, but I'm afraid my friends will bug me if I don't do the bad things they do. Will God watch out for me?

For the LORD watches over the way of the righteous, but the way of the wicked will perish.

PSALM 1:6

2
Help Wanted

I didn't grow up during the Agricultural Revolution and was never surrounded by cornfields or farm animals, but I'm convinced that the reason my parents had seven kids (I'm #5) was so that they could put each of us to work at an early age. I had five sisters and a younger brother, and since I was the oldest boy, my father put tools in my hands as soon as I could hold them. Other kids on the block got to play with toys; I was given a rake.

The only time I can remember work being pleasurable was when I followed my dad around while *he* mowed the lawn. I remember pleading with him, "Pleeeaaasse, Dad, let me mow the lawn! Can I? Can I? Can I, pleeeaasse?" Watching that lawnmower blade rip, chop, flick, and macerate everything in its path, I couldn't wait until I was old enough to wield real pushing power on my own. Little did I know then that my dad was grooming mo, leading me on, waiting for the perfect moment to initiate that life-changing rite of passage of raking leaves and mowing the lawn every Wednesday afternoon.

It all started with a stupid, used, yellow surfboard. I was in the fourth grade, and I thought I wanted to learn how to surf. Wanting to teach me a few lessons about the value of work and how to handle money, my dad offered me a deal that got me a surfboard and him a gardener. The surfboard cost forty dollars, and for one dollar an hour, I could pay it off by cleaning the front and back yards of our home every week. My dad was so excited about his new business operation, he franchised the "Garden Committee" by making similar arrangements with a couple of my older sisters who wanted to buy some stuff of their own but lacked the cash to do so.

Raking leaves, mowing the lawn, and hosing down the driveway got old fast, but I was stuck. Every week, cleaning the yard only took about two hours, so after twenty weeks (five long months), I was eager for early retirement from the Garden Committee. Unfortunately, my dad was out a gardener, so instead of me retiring, he offered to pay me for my services at the same wage of a dollar an hour. I could now spend my money as I pleased, and my dad got a clean garden every week.

When you're young, work looks fun and exciting, but as you get older, for most people, work becomes exactly what it's called: a chore. Work doesn't have to be a chore, though, if you understand its importance and the benefits it offers.

The most obvious reason young people work is for money. Cash. Money enables them to buy stuff they want and do things they want to do. There are other reasons young people work: Some have to work because their family needs help paying bills; some work to avoid spending time with their family; and others work because it gives them a sense of independence and responsibility. Whatever the reason for going out and getting a job as a teenager, having a job ultimately prepares you for what you will spend the rest of your life doing: WORKING!

The Bible is filled with ideas, thoughts, and principles about work and how to handle the money you earn from your job. God is interested in how you perform on your job, whether you are self-employed, unemployed, or work in Missile Deployment. He doesn't care if you're employed by IBM, McDonald's, or Ike's Ice Cube Factory. He is interested in the decisions you make concerning integrity, materialism, customers, honesty, conflicts with coworkers, bosses, money, and paying Uncle Sam his share of your dinero. This chapter works on all sorts of these laborious issues and more. God's Word will give you the practical, helpful advice you need to face the difficulties of being a Christian in the working world. "And whatever you do, whether in word or deed, do it all in the name of the Lord Jesus, giving thanks to God the Father through him" (Col. 3:17).

Working with Bosses

Who's in Charge?

 Let's face one simple fact: When you work for someone else, your job is on the line. Your boss, whether he or she is an Attila the Hun or a soft-as-a-baby's bottom pushover, is the one you report to in your job. A boss's role is not only to hold you accountable to perform a specific task but to see that you do it well. It doesn't matter if you're plucking leaves and lizard guts out of lawn-mower blades or balancing the federal budget, somewhere in the chain of command, somebody created your job because it serves a specific function. As a Christian, how you perform your

job speaks loudly about your faith. If you let everyone at Yazoo Yogurt Shop know that the only real boss in your life is God, but you're not willing to mop dried-up yogurt off the floor, your boss and coworkers will probably wonder if your eternal employer will soon be going out of business. This section will help you develop Christlike attitudes and actions that will show your boss you mean business.

Why can't I tell my boss what I really think of her?

With the tongue we praise our Lord and Father, and with it we curse men, who have been made in God's likeness. Out

He Who Dies with the Most Toys ... Still Dies

Riding the wild, bucking, untameable Wheel of Fortune can knock you on your can before you realize you've been thrown. Pursuing money for the sake of money is like chasing ghosts in the Haunted House at Disneyland: Just when you think you've got your hands on one, it disappears. Chasing a lifestyle of riches, wealth, and shipping crates full of material toys is an empty, vaporous pursuit that can vanish before your very eyes. You are left with nothing. Nada. Zip. Zero.

The Bible tells us not to pursue riches but instead a relationship with God. John was one of Jesus' followers who didn't have much to his name, but he was still a very wealthy man. John wanted other Christians to know about the richness found in a strong relationship with God. He said, "For everything in the world—the cravings of sinful man, the lust of his eyes and the boasting of what he has and does—comes not from the Father but from the world. The world and its desires pass away, but the

(Rich, huh?)

☞

Working with Bosses

of the same mouth come praise and cursing. My brothers, this should not be.

JAMES 3:9–10

My boss is from another country, and we always have communication problems; what should I do?

Everyone should be quick to listen, slow to speak and slow to become angry.

JAMES 1:19

My boss yells at me in front of my coworkers; should I try to get even?

Do not take revenge, my friends, but leave room for God's wrath, for it is written: "It is mine to avenge; I will repay," says the Lord.

ROMANS 12:19

man who does the will of God lives forever" (1 John 2:16–17). You can have the most wonderful toys in all the world—BMX bikes, 4 X 4 Jeeps, jet skis, roller blades, colossal card collections, and ten bright red BMWs filled with beautiful babes, but the Bible says when you take your last breath, you can't take it with you.

Less Is More

Craving. Lusting. Boasting. This three-headed monster can rip, roar, and rear its ugly shadow in your life if you don't allow God's love to tame it. It's capable of destroying your love for God if you let it because it's starving for attention. The Craving-Lusting-Boasting Monster wants only one thing: More and more and more

. . . it's not satisfied with having one pair of roller blades or saving sex for marriage or bragging just a little. This monster wants it all, right now, and will do anything it takes to get its own way. Instead of feeding this fire-breathing dragon who loves the things of this world, John says to focus your attention on loving your heavenly Father. In God's eyes, less is more, because when you desire what God desires, you soon discover that his love is free, and nothing can compare with his love.

Bigger Isn't Better

In this life, the only thing that makes bigger better is a bigger understanding of a truly BIG God who loves you in a very BIG, BIG way. What could be better than living

(It just gets better!!)

☞

forever? Just think about it . . . be a smart shopper . . . compare the two: You could have everything you desire in this world, which will soon pass away, or you could do something really radical, like living out God's will for your life AND live forever. With the world, you may get temporary riches (no promises), which then turn into barf dust when you die. With God, you are unconditionally, 100 percent guaranteed the satisfying richness of his love, peace, and eternal security . . . for free! You tell me—is that a deal or what? Spinning off the Wheel of Fortune is the smartest twist you can ever take with your life. Do you want vowels, Vanna, or a vibrant, growing rich relationship with God that'll last forever?

(That's all!)

My boss is always critical and negative; how can I keep his criticism from affecting my work?

But in your hearts set apart Christ as Lord. Always be prepared to give an answer to everyone who asks you to give the reason for the hope that you have. But do this with gentleness and respect, keeping a clear conscience, so that those who speak maliciously against your good behavior in Christ may be ashamed of their slander.

1 PETER 3:15–16

My boss is unfair and tends to play favorites; how should I react?

A man's wisdom gives him patience; it is to his glory to overlook an offense.

PROVERBS 19:11

My boss makes promises she doesn't keep. Does God ever break his promises?

You know with all your heart and soul that not one of all the good promises the LORD your God gave you has failed. Every promise has been fulfilled; not one has failed.

JOSHUA 23:14

Working with Bosses

My job environment is very stressful. Can I experience God's peace at work?

"Peace I leave with you; my peace I give you. I do not give to you as the world gives. Do not let your hearts be troubled and do not be afraid."

JOHN 14:27

Nobody seems to notice how hard I work; what's the purpose of working hard?

And we pray this in order that you may live a life worthy of the Lord and may please him in every way: bearing fruit in every good work, growing in the knowledge of God.

COLOSSIANS 1:10

My boss forces me to work on Sundays. What can I tell him?

Remember the Sabbath day by keeping it holy.

EXODUS 20:8

Investing in Integrity

Long-term Payoffs

Today a lot of people have said *adios* to integrity instead of *sayonara* to selfishness. Integrity was once a hot item on the market in this country. Things like honesty, keeping your word, and being reliable were the crucial ingredients to secure trust in relationships. That leaves you with a dilemma: Are you going to invest in integrity or splurge on selfishness? Living God's way means being honest—not stealing out of the cash register, ripping off items from work, or cheating on your time card. (I know . . . in the fifth grade I stole money out of the change bowl while selling ice cream in the Valentine Elementary school cafeteria.) Living God's way means making some tough choices, because it's pretty easy to be selfish. Investing in selfishness may have short-term payoffs, but those will depreciate you as a person. Investing in integrity will not only help you learn how to honor God; it'll yield eternal dividends that can't be measured in dollars and cents.

What does God have to say about temptation?

No temptation has seized you except what is common to man. And God is faithful; he will not let you be tempted beyond what you can bear. But when you are tempted, he will also provide a way out so that you can stand up under it.

1 CORINTHIANS 10:13

Would skipping work matter just this once?

The faithless will be fully repaid for their ways, and the good man rewarded for his.

PROVERBS 14:14

Is it really wrong for me not to pay taxes?

Then he said to them, "Give to Caesar what is Caesar's, and to God what is God's."

MATTHEW 22:21

What does God's Word have to say about laziness?

The sluggard craves and gets nothing, but the desires of the diligent are fully satisfied.

PROVERBS 13:4

Other people at work cut corners and I want to do the same. What can help me fight off this temptation?

May integrity and uprightness protect me, because my hope is in you.

PSALM 25:21

I have a friend at work who steals; what should I say to her?

He who has been stealing must steal no longer, but must work, doing something useful with his own hands.

EPHESIANS 4:28A

I'm sick and tired of doing other people's jobs; what should I do?

Better a patient man than a warrior, a man who controls his temper than one who takes a city.

PROVERBS 16:32

Getting Along with Others

Problems at Work

Hatred can be an extremely powerful force that chews on its own chain like a foaming pitbull with rabies. Unleashed, hatred sinks its teeth into others and won't let go until it destroys the very thing it hates. Hatred among people at work can make a good job stink. Right now, you may be working with someone you can't stand. In fact, trouble, strife, conflict, wars, gossip, cruel pranks, anger, problems, jealousy, fits of rage, and hatred are quite common among people who work together. God's Word will teach you how to deal with problems, how to get along with people, and how to respond in difficult situations instead of reacting. Jesus Christ wants us to love our enemies as he loved his enemies. If you're going to hate, hate the things Jesus hates. Hate sin, poverty, and hypocrisy. Not people.

I'm the only Christian at my job; what should I do?

"In the same way, let your light shine before men, that they may see your good deeds and praise your Father in heaven."

MATTHEW 5:16

The people I work with are always telling gross jokes; how can I be different?

Avoid godless chatter, because those who indulge in it will become more and more ungodly.

2 TIMOTHY 2:16

I work on commission, and a coworker is always stealing my customers; what should I do?

Brothers, if someone is caught in a sin, you who are spiritual should restore him gently. But watch yourself, or you also may be tempted.

GALATIANS 6:1

I don't feel like being a Christian at work; what does the Bible say about this?

You need to persevere so that when you have done the will of God, you will receive what he has promised.

HEBREWS 10:36

The people I work with gossip all the time; how can I keep from being tempted to join them?

The words of a gossip are like choice morsels; they go down to a man's inmost parts.

PROVERBS 18:8

My friend makes little adjustments on her time card and tells me to do the same; what does God want me to do?

I know, my God, that you test the heart and are pleased with integrity.

1 CHRONICLES 29:17A

Getting Along with Others

I know I'm not better than anyone else, but what kind of attitude does God want me to have at work?

Serve one another in love.

GALATIANS 5:13C

I got caught lying for a coworker; what does God say about lying?

The LORD detests lying lips, but he delights in men who are truthful.

PROVERBS 12:22

Using Your Friends

Fringe Benefit Friendships

 Getting into the movies for free, buying an expensive pair of shoes at cost, or paying for a scoop of ice cream and getting a monster-sized sundae instead are all creative ways to get stuff from your friends that isn't theirs to give away. In other languages and cultures, it's called stealing or theft. For a lot of teenagers in the United States, it's called "employee discount," or "Don't worry about it," or "Go now! My boss isn't looking!" It's what I call a "fringe benefit" friendship or when your friends know that your job is their ticket to a free ride. That puts you in a difficult situation: Do you give your friends anything they want or do you choose to be a person of integrity? Some businesses allow their employees certain privileges when it comes to giving things away. However, if you don't have permission to give, sell, or discount something, keep your hands off. You could end up in jail by being generous with stuff that isn't yours. Each year, millions of dollars are lost in companies because of employee theft. It's a crime to steal, no matter how small the scoop may be. Having friends steal for you is even a bigger crime. Stealing for friends cheapens friendship and

Living beyond Minimum Wage

Working for minimum wage can be lousy. Living life like minimum wage is even worse. Minimum wage means wiping the gooey sludge under dripping refrigerators, taking out tons of stinking trash, sweeping, painting, mopping, scrubbing, wiping, filling, emptying, and disinfecting every toilet, sink, trash can, and countertop in sight. Grunt labor . . . who needs it? Who wants it? But if you're short on cash and need a job, what else can you do?

If you're like most teenagers, you'd probably like the idea of being the president, CEO, and owner of the company your very first day on the job. Sorry; it ain't gonna happen. The majority of jobs for young people pay minimum wage because most positions at that pay scale do not require prior experience. Wages are usually determined by the type of job and the necessary experience required. Removing toxic waste requires a lot more knowledge and experience than ripping tickets at the entrance of a movie theater. You may not get strange diseases from taking tickets,

(Read on!!)

☞

devalues you as a person. Friends who want stuff and not a quality friendship are basically saying, "I don't care if you lose your job; I'm interested in stuff and not you." Don't live on the fringe.

What should I tell my friends when they ask me to buy them stuff with my employee discount?

My son, if sinners entice you, do not give in to them. If they say, "Come along with us . . . we will get all sorts of valuable things and fill our houses with plunder; throw in your lot with us, and we will share a common purse"—my son, do not go along with them, do not set foot on their paths.

PROVERBS 1:10–11, 13–15

I work at a movie theater, and my friends spend all day hopping from one movie to the next. Is it wrong for me to ignore this problem?

The LORD detests the way of the wicked but he loves those who pursue righteousness.

PROVERBS 15:9

My friends get all the money they want from their folks and I have to work; is it wrong for me to feel jealous?

Using Your Friends

For where you have envy and selfish ambition, there you find disorder and every evil practice.

JAMES 3:16

My friends have jobs that pay really well, and I get minimum wage; how should I feel?

Whoever loves money never has money enough; whoever loves wealth is never satisfied with his income. This too is meaningless.

ECCLESIATES 5:10

I work at an ice cream shop, and my friends give me a hard time if I don't give it to them for free. What can I do?

Bloodthirsty men hate a man of integrity and seek to kill the upright.

PROVERBS 29:10

My Christian friends are always so competitive about who makes more money. How can I help solve this problem?

Command them to do good, to be rich in good deeds, and to be generous and willing to share.

1 TIMOTHY 6:18

A friend of mine wants me to replace a stereo I know he intentionally broke; should I return it for him?

Turn from evil and do good.

PSALM 34:14

but you also won't make a hundred thousand dollars a year. However, if you want to earn more than minimum wage, the quickest way is by letting your employer see a good attitude and your ability to be responsible with whatever job you've been give to do. That'll show your boss you're dependable and more interested in your work than earning an extra buck. In Jesus' words, it means being faithful in the little things before expecting the bigger and better glamorous jobs.

Bosses have enough on their minds without having to remind employees not to hang on the phone or to stop being rude to customers. A lot of teenagers get stuck at minimum wage because their attitudes and actions aren't worth a raise. If you want your boss to notice you when it comes time for a raise, let your job performance speak for itself the day you get hired. Don't sell out for minimal effort at your job, because minimal effort often equals minimum wage.

(That's all!)

Getting a Job

My Parents Made Me Do It

I'll never forget the day my dad took me down to Mac's Coffee Break when I was thirteen years old. "Are you hiring any dishwashers?" he asked as I sarcastically thought, "How did Dad know I'd rather wash dishes all summer instead of going to the beach?" That summer I peeled potatoes, mopped scum off a sticky floor, bused trays filled with cold, half-eaten French toast, runny eggs, ketchup-filled plates, and macerated tuna fish salads. Finishing work at 3:00 in the afternoon, I couldn't wait to run home and jump in the ocean to clean off my sweaty, sticky body. Working at Mac's was a drag. And I only worked two or three days a week.

If your parents want you to get a job, there's a good chance they're trying to teach you some important lessons about money and responsibility. Is God the same way? NO, but his Word contains ideas, principles, lessons, and truths about "parent-enforced" work that can teach you how to live life like it isn't a part-time job.

Why should I have to use my money to pay for my family's needs?

If anyone does not provide for his relatives, and especially for his immediate family, he has denied the faith and is worse than an unbeliever.

1 TIMOTHY 5:8

My parents expect me to get good grades and do well in sports, and now they're pressuring me to get a job. How can I do all this by myself?

We were under great pressure, far beyond our ability to endure, so that we despaired even of life. Indeed, in our hearts

Twenty Ways to Mash Materialism

Here are some great ways to develop a heart that loves God and not stuff.

- Sponsor a Compassion Child.
- Give money to your church.
- Buy a homeless person lunch.
- Give away something that would be really hard to give away.
- Do a Bible study on greed, money, giving, or poverty.
- Write down the things that you want and what you actually need to live.
- Buy groceries for a family in need.
- Have a garage sale and donate the money to a local charity.
- Take a collection in your youth group for a special cause.
- Offer to do chores for an elderly person.
- Visit the sick people in your neighborhood or church.
- Babysit for free the children of a single parent.
- Ask your parents and friends what they think about materialism.
- Research the whole topic of materialism and write a report about it.
- Start a club on campus designed to help the poor.
- Offer to help at a local soup kitchen or thrift store.
- Make two piles in your room (Stuff I need & Stuff I want) and see what you learn.
- Interview a homeless person.
- See what it's like to live without your allowance for one month.

we felt the sentence of death. But this happened that we might not rely on ourselves but on God, who raises the dead.

2 Corinthians 1:8–9

My parents make me work at the family business; how can I keep a positive attitude?

You were taught, with regard to your former way of life, to put off your old self, which is being corrupted by its deceitful desires; to be made new in the attitude of your minds; and

Getting a Job

to put on the new self, created to be like God in true righteousness and holiness.

EPHESIANS 4:22–24

I really need a job, but I can't seem to find one. How can I get my parents to believe me?

Commit to the LORD whatever you do, and your plans will succeed.

PROVERBS 16:3

I'm so tired when I get home from work that I don't have the strength or motivation to do my chores; what should I do?

Look to the LORD and his strength; seek his face always.

PSALM 105:4

My parents promised my uncle I'd work for him without first asking me. How can I tell my uncle I don't want to work for him?

Your own family—even they have betrayed you.

JEREMIAH 12:6

Storing Up Treasures

Material Madness

 A major motivating factor for having a job is to have cash in order to buy stuff. Materialism doesn't motivate all teenagers to work, but it does for a lot. You live in a society that prides itself in buying, owning, keeping, and hoarding stuff that God says will ultimately pass away. When you place too much importance on material things, it's easy to forget what's really important in life. An insatiable desire to hold onto things that break, get old, or get lost is a waste of the precious time you have on this earth. It doesn't take much to be materialistic. Whether your

Storing Up Treasures

dad's a millionaire or you live below the poverty level, materialism begins in the heart because it has to do with loving stuff more than loving God. Do you own your stuff or does your stuff own you?

How can I choose between a new stereo or going on the youth retreat?

"Do not store up for yourselves treasures on earth, where moth and rust destroy, and where thieves break in and steal. But store up for yourselves treasures in heaven, where moth and rust do not destroy, and where thieves do not break in and steal. For where your treasure is, there your heart will be also."

MATTHEW 6:19–21

I tend to love money more than God; what will happen to me?

People who want to get rich fall into temptation and a trap and into many foolish and harmful desires that plunge men into ruin and destruction. For the love of money is a root of all kinds of evil. Some people, eager for money, have wandered from the faith and pierced themselves with many griefs.

1 TIMOTHY 6:9–10

I feel secure by having a lot of material possessions; is this wrong?

But godliness with contentment is great gain. For we brought nothing into the world, and we can take nothing out of it.

1 TIMOTHY 6:6–7

I have a problem with overspending; is this wrong?

"No one can serve two masters. Either he will hate the one and love the other, or he will be devoted to the one and despise the other. You cannot serve both God and Money."

MATTHEW 6:24

How can I keep from comparing myself to my friends who have so much "stuff"?

"Therefore I tell you, do not worry about your life, what you will eat or drink; or about your body, what you will wear. Is not life more important than food, and the body more important than clothes?"

MATTHEW **6:25**

Is it wrong to want to be rich?

Do not be overawed when a man grows rich, when the splendor of his house increases; for he will take nothing with him when he dies, his splendor will not descend with him.

PSALM **49:16–17**

Working on Your Attitude

Your Attitude Stinks

How bad does your attitude smell? Does it penetrate the olfactory nerves of salivating slugs in a seeping sewer? Does it repel everyone who catches a whiff of it? Can your boss smell it the moment he asks you to spray out a few disgusting trash cans? Bad attitudes at work create a lot of hassles: hassles for your coworkers; hassles for your boss; and most of all, hassles for you. Any boss sincerely concerned for his business won't tolerate a teenager whose attitude clearly affects his or her job perform-ance. So what do you do when you've had a lousy day? Are you supposed to show up at work with a big fake smile on your face? What can you do when you know your attitude smells like the bowels of a trash truck? Pray. Take a time out. Pray. Catch your breath and count to a thousand. Pray. Ask for two weeks' paid vacation. Pray.

Talking to God and remembering what his Word says is your only hope. Well, it may not be your only hope, but it certainly is the best. You could also try talking to a friend at work or someone who's willing to listen to how you're feeling. But when

64 *Working on Your Attitude*

you talk to God, you've got the attention of your Creator. Whether your attitude stinks or not, he cares about you. Sure, even God hates the smell of a rotten attitude, but he can tolerate it more than most people. He's got the strength and power to help you change it if you're willing to let him. Let his Word remind you that, even at work, he wants you to have the attitude of Jesus Christ.

How can I keep from hating work?

And whatever you do, whether in word or deed, do it all in the name of the Lord Jesus, giving thanks to God the Father through him.

COLOSSIANS 3:17

I'm always complaining at work. I know I need to change, but what does God say?

Do everything without complaining or arguing.

PHILIPPIANS 2:14

How can I keep from being lazy on the job?

All hard work brings a profit, but mere talk leads only to poverty.

PROVERBS 14:23

Why do I have to do all the grunt work?

It is better, if it is God's will, to suffer for doing good than for doing evil.

1 PETER 3:17

I can't stand working on sale days. What type of qualities should I try to develop when I'm being tested?

But the fruit of the Spirit is . . . patience, kindness, goodness, . . . and self-control.

GALATIANS 5:22–23

How can I make my work meaningful?

So whether you eat or drink or whatever you do, do it all for the glory of God.

1 CORINTHIANS 10:31

What should I do when I'm forced to be nice to a customer I can't stand?

Serve wholeheartedly, as if you were serving the Lord, not men.

EPHESIANS 6:7

How should I respond when a customer accuses me of being rude to her?

A gentle answer turns away wrath, but a harsh word stirs up anger.

PROVERBS 15:1

I have a hard time helping people who treat me as if I'm their personal slave. What can I do to be more like Christ?

But just as you excel in everything—in faith, in speech, in knowledge, in complete earnestness and in your love for us— see that you also excel in this grace of giving.

2 CORINTHIANS 8:7

What type of attitude did Christ have when it came to serving others?

"Now that I, your Lord and Teacher, have washed your feet, you also should wash one another's feet. I have set you an example that you should do as I have done for you."

JOHN 13:14–15

Working on Your Attitude

Crosstraining Your Faith
Crosstraining Your Faith
Crosstraining Your Faith
Crosstraining Your Faith
Crosstraining Your Faith
Crosstraining Your Faith
Crosstraining Your Faith
Crosstraining Your Faith
Crosstraining Your Faith
Crosstraining Your Faith

3

Crosstraining Your Faith

Barbed wire. Suck sand and stay low. Thirty-foot cargo nets. *Slip and you will die.* Climbing walls. *Without safety nets.* Rope climbs; rope ladders; rope swings. *Rope burns.* Rolling logs. *Don't land in the middle.* Four-story towers with no stairs. *How you get up is your problem.* A one-hundred-fifty-foot rope connected from the four-story tower to a ten-foot pole. *You go first. No, really, I insist!* Monkey bars. *A little bit harder than the ones at the playground.* Ten-foot walls; twelve-foot walls; fourteen-foot walls. *Bring a ladder.*

Does all this reading make you tired? *Wait until you're on the course.* Deep sand. *It's what you run in.* Hurdles. *Crippling hurdles.* Log jumps; log stumps. *The kind that thump.* Wood slides. *Splinters included.* Want a stretcher? *Keep going, soldier; you're not finished!* Throw in an extra set of gymnastic bars, a beast-like metal contraption called the "weaver," a few more logs to slip, slide, and run over, add a dousing in the Pacific Ocean, powder yourself like a donut in the dirt, run three miles in deep sand, top it off with fifty pushups, and you've just completed *THE MOTHER OF ALL OBSTACLE COURSES!* Welcome to the Navy S.E.A.L. Team obstacle course on Coronado Island, San Diego.

I got my first and last shot at this sucker a few years ago. A good friend of mine was a Navy S.E.A.L., and I called him to see if I could bring some students down from our youth group. We were having our summer camp nearby, and I figured an afternoon on the obstacle course would either bury them or bury me.

Over thirty students loaded the vans eager to test their strength and stamina. At that point, nobody told them their worst nightmare was about to give birth. We arrived at the course. We saw the course. We loaded back in the vans figuring we had the wrong one. This one wasn't built for humans. This course was built for the Terminator.

After a couple hours of jumping, falling, thumping, gasping, burning, sliding, grabbing, pulling, screaming, and nursing our war wounds, we all made it out alive. Barely. Rocky Brown got about twenty feet down the rope slide and decided to flip over like an opossum hanging in a tree. He only had a hundred and thirty feet to go. Upside down. Charity Landreth redefined the word *courage* and glided down the rope slide like a snake slithering down a branch. *Hasta la vista, baby.*

If you're a civilian like the rest of us, to complete the course takes about, oh, let's say . . . one to two hours. If you're a S.E.A.L., the first time you do the course, you need to do it in under eleven minutes. Each week you need to beat your time or you'll be sorry you didn't. Really sorry. The S.E.A.L. trainers take their job very seriously. They're out to train one of the most elite forces

Crosstraining Your Faith

in the armed services. Forget about what you've seen in the movie theaters. We don't know what they really do, but you can be certain about one thing: A Navy S.E.A.L. is the ultimate crosstrainer.

A person who crosstrains is someone who practices different sports to develop strength and stamina in various muscle groups. Crosstraining adds creativity to workouts, increases overall conditioning, and eliminates boring repetition found in training for only one sport. Crosstraining works. It strengthens weaknesses to improve the overall performance of the athlete.

For Christian athletes, crosstraining is essential. A football player doesn't just lift weights. A Christian doesn't just pray. A baseball player does more than catch fly balls. A Christian does more than just talk about his or her faith. Crosstraining strengthens an athlete's physical condition. For Christians, getting in spiritual shape strengthens and prepares them to be who God designed them to be. In Paul's letter to Timothy, he said, "Train yourself to be godly. For physical training is of some value, but godliness has value for all things, holding promise for both the present life and the life to come" (1 Tim. 4:7-8). Paul and Timothy grew up in a culture like ours where athletics was a key part of life. Paul knew the importance of physical training to prepare an athlete for competition. He also saw that godliness had tremendous value for anyone willing to follow God's training program.

Teenagers who crosstrain their faith by participating in God's training program have an incredible opportunity to use their athletic abilities to share their faith. Sad, but true, sports have a bigger following than God.

Students who practice their faith on the field can let their friends know where their abilities and strength come from. I've seen a lot of high school athletes with Philippians 4:13 on their letterman's jacket or cheerleading uniform: "I can do everything through him who gives me strength." Not even a muscle-building protein drink offers that type of strength.

God wants to use you, on your campus, in your sport, to show others who he is. It doesn't matter if you win or lose, strike out or miss a shot, Jesus wants you to finish the race you've started. He wants you to someday cross his finish line and say, "I have fought the good fight, I have finished the race, I have kept the faith" (2 Tim. 4:7).

Ruining Your Game

An Athlete's Foot Attitude

 It smells. It reeks. Its stench is stronger than an exploded septic tank. That smell is a bad attitude, and we've all had one before: throwing tennis rackets, golf clubs, and helmets; shot putting bowling balls after hurling three gutterballs in a row; having tantrums like a two-year-old or a professional tennis player.

A bad attitude can ruin your game. It can also ruin your teammates' game and cause you to lose the whole match. Then you won't be the only one with the bad attitude. Bad attitudes spread like an oil spill, staining and ruining everything in their path. Okay, so you're having a bad day. Everyone does once in a while, but before your attitude heads downwind, think of how your attitude makes others feel. You're stressed out; are you going to make everyone else upset too? Take a time-out. Go get a drink. There's nothing you can do about the free throw you just missed. But you can change your attitude. Try it. It'll make a big difference, and you'll enjoy your game a lot more.

I've tried to talk to a teammate about his temper; why won't he listen to me?

Do not make friends with a hot-tempered man, do not associate with one easily angered, or you may learn his ways and get yourself ensnared.

PROVERBS 22:24–25

God has given me a lot of athletic ability, but how should I handle all the praise I get?

When pride comes, then comes disgrace, but with humility comes wisdom.

PROVERBS 11:2

My coach tells me that I'd be more "coachable" if I would change my negative attitude; is he right?

Getting Your Mouth in Shape

For some athletes, training the tongue can be the most difficult muscle group to get in shape. It's so easy to let that little, wet hunk of muscle slip a few nasty words right past your teeth. Keeping control of what you say on the court isn't always easy. Why do we let our tongues say things that can lead to embarrassment, hurt feelings, harsh looks, team disintegration, and yellow cards? The tongue is an indicator, a sort of scoreboard of what's going on inside our hearts and minds. When Jesus spoke about the tongue, he also was speaking about the heart: "For out of the overflow of the heart the mouth speaks" (Matt. 12:34). When

(Stop talking and read on!!)

☞

we're not performing the way we think we should or if our opponent is being a jerk, it's easy to let our emotions take control. Anger, resentment, rage, fear, and worry build up inside our hearts because we don't want to look lame or look like a loser. Brewing inside us like the innards of a volcano, this molten lava mush of explosive feelings looks for the quickest and easiest escape route . . . %#!@$!!

Spouting off can get you benched, kicked out of the game, or cause you to lose your concentration even more than you already have. What are some ways to keep your tongue in your mouth and your mind on your game?

- **Pregame prep:** Think about your attitude, the game, and how you want to act before you get on the court. Ask God to help you watch what you say.
- **Game partner:** Ask a friend, particularly a Christian friend, to be praying for you as you play. Ask him or her to help you keep your tongue in shape. Before you compete, pray together about setting an example for Christ.
- **Scripture focus:** Memorize a favorite Scripture verse to think about during the breaks between plays. Suggested verses: Philippians 3:14, Psalm 118:14, Hebrews 12:2, 2 Timothy 4:7, 1 Corinthians 9:24, Philippians 4:13.

(One to go!!)

☞

Pride only breeds quarrels, but wisdom is found in those who take advice.

PROVERBS 13:10

What can I say to this guy on my team who thinks he's so great?

If anyone thinks he is something when he is nothing, he deceives himself.

GALATIANS 6:3

What should I do if I can't stand the coach?

Do everything without complaining or arguing.

PHILIPPIANS 2:14

How can God's Word change my attitude?

For the word of God is living and active. Sharper than any double-edged sword, it penetrates even to dividing soul and spirit, joints and marrow; it judges the thoughts and attitudes of the heart.

HEBREWS 4:12

I don't understand: Why is the best player on my team the biggest jerk?

An unfriendly man pursues selfish ends; he defies all sound judgment.

PROVERBS 18:1

Ruining Your Game

Being a Team Player

Teamwork

 Ball hogs. Prima donnas. Glory seekers. People who can't be team players make awful team-mates because they're only looking out for them-selves. They think the team exists to make them look good. If the team doesn't look good and plays like a bunch of third-graders, they think it's someone else's fault. Have you ever felt like saying to this type of character, "You're not being nice! I'm taking my ball and going home!"

Being a team player is a very important part of living out your faith on the court, track, field, or gym. People will see Christ in you if you look to both their interests and the team's best interests. No one wants to be a loser, but people who can't be team players are already on the losing team. Being a team player doesn't mean you have to be a rah-rah cheer-leader or mascot. You just need to be willing to give your best, be humble, and do whatever it takes to make the team look good (without cheating, of course!). People on the court and off the court are looking for a reason to live. You can help put God in their lives by putting him first, them second, and your-self third. When you put yourself in third place, that's first place in God's eyes. That's the type of team player God wants on his team.

How can I keep from getting jealous when my teammates play better than me?

Each one should test his own actions. Then he can take pride in himself, without comparing himself to somebody else.

GALATIANS 6:4

How can I be a better encourager to my teammates?

Being a Team Player   73

- **Apologize:** Okay, so everything you just did to avoid shooting off your mouth didn't work. Own up to it and say you're sorry to God and anyone else you may have hurt or offended. Saying you're sorry isn't a sign of weakness but a Christlike example of honesty and integrity.
- **Be patient:** Change doesn't happen overnight. Just as it takes months to get in excellent shape, it takes a long time to change bad habits. Spend some time reading James 3 and ask God to give you the desire and strength to be his person on and off the court. Bench pressing your tongue into shape can weigh you down and make you sore. But like all workouts, out of soreness comes strength.

(That's all!)

As iron sharpens iron, so one man sharpens another.

PROVERBS 27:17

There's a lot of squabbling on my team; how can I make a difference?

Let us not become conceited, provoking and envying each other.

GALATIANS 5:26

How can I encourage my teammates so they'll see Christ in me?

My purpose is that they may be encouraged in heart and united in love, so that they may have the full riches of complete understanding, in order that they may know the mystery of God, namely, Christ.

COLOSSIANS 2:2

How can I demonstrate God's love to my teammates?

No one has ever seen God; but if we love one another, God lives in us and his love is made complete in us.

1 JOHN 4:12

Being a Team Player

My team is great on the court but lousy off the court; what should we do?

Finally, all of you, live in harmony with one another; be sympathetic, love as brothers, be compassionate and humble.

1 Peter 3:8

There's a lot of fighting on my team; how can I keep from getting stuck in the middle?

I appeal to you, brothers, in the name of our Lord Jesus Christ, that all of you agree with one another so that there may be no divisions among you and that you may be perfectly united in mind and thought.

1 Corinthians 1:10

Hanging in There

Perseverance

You don't need to be a great athlete to go out for cross country. All you need is two legs, a set of lungs, a knack for pain, and a stretcher at the finish line. I coached cross country for three years at Dana Hills High School in Dana Point, California. I really didn't know much about the sport. But I knew the head coach. He gave me a group of sophomore guys and a lesson in life: "In order to cross the finish line, you've got to be moving." It doesn't matter how fast you are or how slow you go, but if you want to finish the race, you need to be moving.

The same is true for following Jesus Christ. The Christian life is a race. The path is straight and narrow, the goal is Jesus Christ, and the prize is eternal life. It's a race filled with adventure, hills and valleys, pressures, and sideaches. Whatever you do, don't give up. Giving up is always an option, the easiest thing to do, the quickest way to the drinking fountain. But when you get in the habit of giving up, quitting becomes easier and easier. Pretty soon you become numb to what it means to keep a commitment. You may have all sorts of reasons for quitting, but the only one who loses is you. God can give you all the energy, strength, power, courage, endurance, and oxygen you need to hang in there, but even he won't keep you from quitting. He's spread the tape across the finish and is cheering you along the whole way. When you feel like giving up, give yourself up to God and trust him to get you to the finish.

What should I do when I feel like quitting?

I have fought the good fight, I have finished the race, I have kept the faith.

2 TIMOTHY 4:7

I can't understand why God allowed me to get injured right before a big game; what good is supposed to come out of this?

Not only so, but we also rejoice in our sufferings, because we know that suffering produces perseverance; perseverance, character; and character, hope.

ROMANS 5:3–4

I'm not a very good athlete; how can I keep from getting discouraged?

Therefore, since we are surrounded by such a great cloud of witnesses, let us throw off everything that hinders and the sin that so easily entangles, and let us run with perseverance the race marked out for us.

HEBREWS 12:1

My coach knows I'm a Christian, and he says things just to get a reaction out of me; what should I do?

Consider it pure joy, my brothers, whenever you face trials of many kinds, because you know that the testing of your faith

Hanging in There

develops perseverance. Perseverance must finish its work so that you may be mature and complete, not lacking anything.

JAMES 1:2–4

How can I be a good witness to my teammates?

For this very reason, make every effort to add to your faith goodness; and to goodness, knowledge; and to knowledge, self-control; and to self-control, perseverance; and to perseverance, godliness; and to godliness, brotherly kindness; and to brotherly kindness, love.

2 PETER 1:5–7

Does it matter that my coach doesn't see how hard I'm trying?

We continually remember before our God and Father your work produced by faith, your labor prompted by love, and your endurance inspired by hope in our Lord Jesus Christ.

1 THESSALONIANS 1:3

It's really hard living like a Christian around my teammates; what should I do?

However, I consider my life worth nothing to me, if only I may finish the race and complete the task the Lord Jesus has given me—the task of testifying to the gospel of God's grace.

ACTS 20:24

Feeling like a Failure

The Weight of Insecurity

I don't care what anyone says, but everyone, at one time or another, loses at something. It could be a game, competition, relationship, test score, or driving test. Everyone fails. However, there's a big difference between failing and losing. You could lose the best match of your life knowing you played your very best. That's not failure. Or you could win an easy competition and feel like a complete loser. How you view losing and failing often determines how you feel about yourself. A successful athlete may lose a lot of matches but learn from each loss. That's not failure. That's progress. On the other hand, a great athlete could win almost every event he or she competes in but still feel like a failure inside.

God understands how you feel when you lose. He also knows what's going on inside of you when you feel like a failure. He knows how your self-esteem can be too closely tied to your win/loss record. That's why he wants you to find your security in him, not in your trophies or medals. He's more interested in how you feel about yourself and your friendship with him than any school records you hope to set. The pressure to succeed can squish your self-esteem and leave you pinned under the weight of insecurity. God's Word says that we are more than conquerors through him who loved us. In Jesus Christ, you are not a failure or a loser. Only a winner.

I blew the winning shot, and none of my teammates will talk to me; who can I turn to?

Guard my life and rescue me; let me not be put to shame, for I take refuge in you.

PSALM 25:20

I get really depressed when I lose; what should I do?

Therefore we do not lose heart. Though outwardly we are wasting away, yet inwardly we are being renewed day by day.

2 CORINTHIANS 4:16

Feeling like a Failure

Did Jesus ever feel like a loser?

Consider him who endured such opposition from sinful men, so that you will not grow weary and lose heart.

HEBREWS 12:3

I'm not playing like I used to, and I can't understand why. Will God help me?

My flesh and my heart may fail, but God is the strength of my heart and my portion forever.

PSALM 73:26

I feel like a complete failure when I lose. Does God love me even when I fail?

I will maintain my love to him forever, and my covenant with him will never fail.

PSALM 89:28

I'm in a slump; will God pull me out?

But the LORD is with me like a mighty warrior.

JEREMIAH 20:11

I don't want winning to become more important than my relationship with God; what should I do?

"The man who loves his life will lose it, while the man who hates his life in this world will keep it for eternal life."

JOHN 12:25

How can I have a good attitude when I lose?

Because the Sovereign LORD helps me, I will not be disgraced. Therefore have I set my face like flint, and I know I will not be put to shame.

ISAIAH 50:7

Getting Focused

Don't Look Back

 Missed shot. Dropped ball. Incomplete pass. Out of bounds. So what are you going to do now? You just blew it. Everybody was watching. You're embarrassed.

Dwelling on a bad shot gets you nowhere. I know you've heard it before, but it's true. Look forward, not backward. Too much energy is wasted on thinking how you just blew it. It ruins your concentration for what's still happening in the game. Looking back produces frustration, which can make you mess up again. The only value in looking back is to see what you did wrong, think about it, learn from it, and then drop-kick it out of your mind.

Blowing it with God also isn't an easy thing to forget. Looking at your mistakes can get you focused on yourself instead of God's forgiveness. When you break God's heart by doing something wrong, the best thing to do is admit your sin, ask him to forgive you, accept his forgiveness, and turn from committing the same mistake again. God doesn't look back, and he doesn't want you to look back either. He wants to share his friendship with you. God forgets your sin. He doesn't dwell on your past. His forgiveness drop-kicks your mistakes as far as east is to west. That's a long way.

How can I forget about my bad performance in the last meet?

"Forget the former things; do not dwell on the past. See, I am doing a new thing! Now it springs up; do you not perceive it? I am making a way in the desert and streams in the wasteland."

ISAIAH 43:18–19

My bad attitude caused us to lose last night; will God forgive me?

Getting Focused

From the Jaws of Death

The Story of Michael Young
and Wave Riders Against Drugs

Thundering a couple miles off the coast of Maui, "Jaws" is a dangerous, high-adrenaline surfing spot known for huge (we're talking absolutely humongous) waves. Appropriately named, Jaws has a churning, foaming mouth with a bite size reaching seven stories high. Armed with high-speed Wetbikes, tow ropes, and state-of-the-art surfboards, a nucleus of the best big-wave riders in the world known as "power surfers" take on the death-defying thrill of surfing Jaws without getting eaten alive. With the advent of tow-in surfing at spots like Jaws, surfers are now taking this sport to new levels at places such as the Cortez Bank off the coast of California.

On the nearby island of Oahu and across the Pacific in San Clemente, California, a group of professional surfers, ex-drug addicts, and recovering alcoholics take on a different sort of beast . . . one that has devoured more lives in this country than the big wave spots could ever hope to consume in a thousand years. This animal is more subtle: It comes in the form of marijuana, cocaine, LSD, heroin, crystal meth, alcohol, psychedelic mushrooms, and yes, even cigarettes.

The powerful undertow of peer pressure, drugs and alcohol, and poor decision making can be deadly, and this is the message presented by W.R.A.D. (Wave Riders Against Drugs). W.R.A.D. drops in at public and Christian schools loaded with free surfing merchandise, substance abuse education, and a drug-free message from professional surfers and others who have escaped a lifestyle of drugs, gangs, and prison. Led by Hawaiian surfer and professional musician, Michael Young, the story of W.R.A.D. and its impact upon thousands of teenagers in Hawaii and California is a truly radical tale of how God can free anyone from the deadly jaws of drugs and alcohol.

Book'em

Mike Young was born and raised in Hawaii. His father was a police officer who worked on Beat 40, the shantytown area of Chinatown popular among Navy sailors for its bars, strip joints, and prostitution.

His first experience with drugs was at age thirteen when he began smoking cigarettes just to be cool. Michael soon went from using cigarettes to smoking marijuana. Growing up in the '60s with the popularity of psychedelic drugs, Michael reasoned

(What a story!!)

☞

"I, even I, am he who blots out your transgressions, for my own sake, and remembers your sins no more."

ISAIAH 43:25

I used to pray before games, but now I don't even include God in anything. Does he still care about me?

The LORD appeared to us in the past, saying: "I have loved you with an everlasting love; I have drawn you with loving-kindness."

JEREMIAH 31:3

I started a fight that got our team disqualified; will I be forgiven for that?

When we were overwhelmed by sins, you forgave our transgressions.

PSALM 65:3

I recently made a commitment to Christ, but I have a hard time living like a Christian on the court. How can I know I'm still a Christian?

But because of his great love for us, God, who is rich in mercy, made us alive with Christ even when we were dead in transgressions—it is by grace you have been saved.

EPHESIANS 2:4–5

I got angry and made a fool of myself at my game last night; is God angry with me?

Remember not the sins of my youth and my rebellious ways; according to your love remember me, for you are good, O LORD.

PSALM 25:7

I used to be known for being a team leader, but now I'm a nobody. Can I still make a difference on my team for God?

Getting Focused

that drugs were just the thing to do. Eventually, he became what he calls "a very incorrigible teenager." Because his parents were having such a hard time with him, they shipped him off to California to finish high school, where his drug use pulled him into the dark and murky depths of LSD and other psychedelic drugs.

After finishing high school, in order to avoid the Vietnam draft, Mike went back to Hawaii to pursue a career in (of all things) law enforcement. Since his older brother had already joined the police force, Mike decided to also follow in his father's footsteps. As a police officer, he first worked in "Receiving" at the Honolulu Police Department, where suspected criminals were booked, fingerprinted, and placed in a cell. From there, he hit the streets and worked the same turf, Beat 40, that his father and brother patrolled. But, after four years as a police officer, Mike's interest in becoming a professional musician overshadowed his desire to spend the rest of his life pounding the pavement. He left the force and eventually became the type of person he used to arrest.

Let's Make a Deal

Within a few years, Mike developed a successful career as a professional musician in Hawaii's most famous resorts. Before long his night life career boomeranged him back into drugs. From singing in hotel bars and using drugs with friends, Mike moved to dealing cocaine and marijuana. Small amounts led to larger amounts and large amounts led to even bigger amounts. Mike asked a friend to fly to California to pick up a kilo of cocaine, but that wasn't the only thing his friend brought back.

Unknown to Mike, his friend had been arrested in California, and the federal drug enforcement agents convinced him to turn Mike in . . . which he did.

Writing on the Wall

After being arrested for trafficking drugs across state lines, Mike was escorted to the Honolulu Police Department, the same place he used to work. He was booked, fingerprinted, and placed in the same cell he used to put prisoners.

Seeing the words "Jesus loves you" on the wall of the cell, Mike got on his knees and began to pray, offering his life to Christ. Mike's troubles obviously didn't drift away like a late afternoon tide. Based upon what his friend told the federal agents, Mike was facing a looooooong time in prison. After two days in jail, Mike posted bail and didn't waste any time getting radical for Christ.

While he was in the cell, the word *WRAD* flashed in his brain. He ignored it for a while because he didn't know what it meant, but later it came to him: *Wave Riders Against Drugs.* God wanted him to tell his story to kids in school.

Paddling Out

Within two months of getting arrested, Mike began visiting public schools to tell his story. A whole series of people—many of them professional surfers—streamed into Mike's life to take this anti-drug message to the schools.

(There's more!!)

☞

For this very reason, make every effort to add to your faith goodness; and to goodness, knowledge; and to knowledge, self-control; and to self-control, perseverance; and to perseverance, godliness; and to godliness, brotherly kindness; and to brotherly kindness, love. For if you possess these qualities in increasing measure, they will keep you from being ineffective and unproductive in your knowledge of our Lord Jesus Christ.

2 PETER 1:5–8

Being on God's Team

Stiff Competition

I hate getting creamed. I'll never forget the time I tried out to be a beach lifeguard in South Orange County. I'm not a fish by nature, and I was never a competitive swimmer; let's just say I was up against an army of studs. I was a senior in high school and spent a whole semester in the pool preparing for the try-outs. Two weeks before the tryouts I got the flu and was in bed for a week and a half. The day of the tryouts came, I hadn't swam in two weeks, and I was in for a dunking. There were only sixty guys trying out for ten spots. *Only sixty!* I figured my chances of making the cut were about one in sixty. Even though I was sick, out of shape, and out of hope, I still wanted to compete. Or should I say, I wanted to watch the other swimmers compete while I dog paddled behind in their jet wash. The race was a half-mile run, half-mile swim, half-mile run. I did well. I finished. Last. Dead last. Dead and last.

Stiff competition is a part of life. There's always going to be someone or some team that is better, stronger, faster, or able to throw locomotives in a single bound. When you're faced with stiff competition and have that gut level feeling that you know you're going to lose, then you've got the advantage. Why? Because that's when the stronger team kicks back and figures

Being on God's Team

Due to a backlog of criminal cases, it took three years for Mike to be sentenced. In the meantime, W.R.A.D. kept growing and growing. By sponsoring surfing competitions and visiting schools, W.R.A.D. established itself as a creative ministry with a positive message for young people.

Judgment Day

When the day of sentencing came, the federal courtroom was packed with people who showed up to support Mike. The judge congratulated Mike on the W.R.A.D. program and his positive contribution to the state of Hawaii. Several people testified on Mike's behalf, but n-e-v-e-r-t-h-e-l-e-s-s, the prosecuting attorney said that Mike was still guilty of trafficking cocaine and to impose no sentence would send the wrong message to the kids of Hawaii.

Before sentencing Mike, the judge asked if he had anything to say. Mike replied that the day he got arrested was the worst day of his life, but it became the most wonderful day because he gave his heart to the Lord Jesus. Mike was facing eight to ten years in federal prison, but instead the judge sentenced him to only two years.

While Mike served his time in federal prison, the W.R.A.D. Hawaii coordinator kept W.R.A.D.'s anti-drug message alive in schools. Mike was eventually released from prison and returned to his role as the founder and director of W.R.A.D.

W.R.A.D. Takes Off

Mike moved to the mainland to bring W.R.A.D.'s drug-free message to California's schools. Based in San Clemente, Mike and his speaking team of professional surfers and recovering addicts present a persuasive and very cool message to elementary and teenage students. Professional surfers grab the attention of teenage surf addicts. Hard-hitting stories about the real consequences of drug abuse from former drug addicts and alcoholics leave students with Gumby eyeballs.

What makes W.R.A.D.'s presentation receive such a positive response from students is their low-key approach. In the short time W.R.A.D. has been in California, over 13,000 kids have received its "surfing and drugs don't mix" message.

As W.R.A.D. continues to do battle against the beast of drug abuse by helping young people to stay drug-free, it has aggressive plans to push into other states and overseas. "Kids today are hurting. They are living with more stress and problems than ever before. I am convinced they need positive role models to help them make good decisions with their lives," says Mike.

From overcoming the monster waves of drug and alcohol abuse to giving kids a message of hope and purpose, this one soul surfer has truly been transformed. W.R.A.D. is making a radical difference in thousands of young people's lives. It's pretty amazing when you think about it: Mike Young doesn't even own a tow rope.

(That's all!)

they'd sweat more in the shower than competing against you. Now is the time to give it all you've got. You've got nothing to lose! Few people perform best against an easy opponent. The majority of people excel against someone who challenges all their abilities. Stiff competition is nothing to be afraid of because the Bible promises that you've got the God of the universe on your team. That doesn't mean he's going to flip the scoreboard in your favor when no one's looking. You have his presence and his strength to help you do your best. He's the One molding and shaping your character as you learn how to act, think, and be more like Christ on and off the court. If you're on God's team, you're going to be hard to beat.

Our team is going to get killed; do we need to be afraid?

Do not be afraid; do not be discouraged. Go out to face them tomorrow, and the LORD will be with you.

2 CHRONICLES 20:17

It's easy for me to train for my sport, but why is it so hard for me to spend time alone with God?

Everyone who competes in the games goes into strict training. They do it to get a crown that will not last; but we do it to get a crown that will last forever.

1 CORINTHIANS 9:25

Winning is so important to me that I'm often tempted to cheat in order to win; how can I overcome this?

Similarly, if anyone competes as an athlete, he does not receive the victor's crown unless he competes according to the rules.

2 TIMOTHY 2:5

Whenever I make the finals of a tournament and ask God to give me a victory, will he always give me one?

Being on God's Team

The horse is made ready for the day of battle, but victory rests with the LORD.

PROVERBS 21:31

Where can I find peace when I'm facing a big match?

All those gathered here will know that it is not by sword or spear that the LORD saves; for the battle is the LORD's.

1 SAMUEL 17:47

What attitude should I have when I face an opponent I've lost to before?

"For I am the LORD, your God, who takes hold of your right hand and says to you, Do not fear; I will help you."

ISAIAH 41:13

I don't get to play much in games; was all my training really worth it?

But I said, "I have labored to no purpose; I have spent my strength in vain and for nothing. Yet what is due me is in the LORD's hand, and my reward is with my God."

ISAIAH 49:4

Developing Discipline
Remote Control

Clicking the channel changer is a wonderful feeling. It's so easy, so painless, so natural. It doesn't cause blisters, sore arms, bruised shins, or aching backs. Remote control is one of the technological wonders of modern society. It's kept us in the couch, comfortable and warm, like a bear in hibernation.

Flipping the channel may work for watching your favorite program. But living by remote control, avoiding the pain and

Totally Intense

"I want to die," Maria whispered to herself as she sat in her lonely, gray apartment in Sydney, Australia. Effortlessly, the words slid off her tongue. Like a steady, advancing troop, the secret dark thoughts of her heart marched forward to command the anguish out of her mouth. An invisible army of pain trampled what little was left inside her.

Maria sat at the kitchen table and stared at the furniture in a hypnotic gaze.

Bosnia. The war. It seemed so long ago. Thousands of miles away. Yet, the battles raged on, the atrocities continued, the political maneuverings of the Serbs, Croats, and the Muslims, the ethnic cleansing. Nothing had changed. Everything had changed.

Alone at the table, Maria whispered the four words again.

I want to die.

Maria's Story

When you wake up tomorrow morning, thank God you're not Maria. Few, if any, Americans will ever witness the brutality and butchery of war like Maria did. If you're wondering why Maria wanted to die, listen to her story.

Maria lived in a small village in Bosnia, Herzegovina. As the battles between the Serbs, Croats, and Muslims stormed into

(Don't stop now!!)

☞

purpose of discipline, creates more chaos than comfort. A lot of athletes do things just because a coach tells them to, but they never develop any personal disciplines of their own. That's remote control living.

Discipline comes from the word *disciple* which means *learner.* Someone who disciplines himself or herself in any area of their life is "learning" how to live. Discipline happens in all sorts of ways: Getting to practice on time; taking the nets down before your coach has to tell you to; holding your tongue when you feel like cussing; keeping promises; eating right; reading the Bible regularly; accepting pain before pleasure.

A good friend once asked me, "Do you want to live with the pain of discipline or the agony of regret?" That's a good way to look at life. Many of us live life saying to ourselves, "I should've, could've, would've . . ." The pain of discipline keeps us learning what God has in store for us. We become life-long learners instead of life-long losers. Yes, discipline is painful, but it yields great rewards. Turn on discipline and turn off the tube. Click!

How can I get through difficult practices?

No discipline seems pleasant at the time, but painful. Later on, however, it produces a harvest of righteousness and peace for those who have been trained by it.

HEBREWS 12:11

Can I be a great tennis player without working for it?

The sluggard craves and gets nothing, but the desires of the diligent are fully satisfied.

PROVERBS 13:4

How can I be as strong a Christian as I am an athlete?

Train yourself to be godly.

1 TIMOTHY 4:7

The people on my team never take practice seriously; what can I say to them?

The fear of the LORD is the beginning of knowledge, but fools despise wisdom and discipline.

PROVERBS 1:7

How can I help my team instead of hurt it?

He who heeds discipline shows the way to life, but whoever ignores correction leads others astray.

PROVERBS 10:17

her hometown, her husband was killed by the Serb forces. When the Serb army seized control of the village, Maria's two sons were murdered as well.

Fleeing the village with her two daughters, Maria headed north for safety. After a couple hundred miles of travel on foot and scavenging for food along the way, Maria and her daughters were apprehended by Serb forces. Like many other Bosnian women before her, Maria watched helplessly as the Serb soldiers sadistically raped and then shot her two girls to death.

Leaving her to starve to death or become a wandering target for a bored sniper, the soldiers let Maria go on her way. Determined to escape her war-ravaged country, Maria struggled another two hundred miles to safety until she finally arrived at a refugee camp near the Italian border. From there, she sought assistance from an international refugee relocation ministry that found her a place to live "down under" in Sydney, Australia.

Maria had never been outside of Bosnia. The only people she knew in Australia were the people who were trying to help her. Even then, Maria could barely communicate with those who knew so little of her pain. Now, after months of running from war, rape, murder, shellings, and sniper fire, alone in a peaceful, faraway country, Maria wanted to die.

Why would someone want to die after living through such danger and life-threatening tension? I think the answer lies not only in the intense desperation

(One more!!)

How can I keep from getting angry when my coach tries to tell me what to do?

Whoever loves discipline loves knowledge, but he who hates correction is stupid.

PROVERBS 12:1

Why do we have hard workouts if we're just going to lose anyway?

Endure hardship as discipline; God is treating you as sons. For what son is not disciplined by his father?

HEBREWS 12:7

Concentrating on Christ

Totally Focused

A personal commitment to Jesus Christ gives you an edge over your competition. God created you with physical, mental, social, and spiritual capacities so you could know him and involve him in every area of your life. He created you for himself. Not the other way around. Knowing Jesus Christ won't necessarily make you a better athlete, but it will give you access to the One with all power, all strength, all endurance, and all creativity. Jesus Christ can help you focus your concentration on him instead of yourself. In the struggle and pressure of competition, you can pray to the God who hears all your prayers and who cares about you.

Jesus is totally focused on you, and he wants you totally focused on him. The Bible says there is strength in the name of the Lord. That includes any type of strength you need. If God made every single bone in your body, how difficult can it be for him to give you strength when you ask for it in his name? Some people ask for strength just because they want to win meets or games. That's not being totally focused. You can be totally focused in whatever you do when you first focus on Christ.

Concentrating on Christ

and grief over losing
her whole family but also in the
absence of tension Maria experienced
in a quiet, lonely apartment.
You see, when Maria was running, struggling,
desperately fleeing for her life, she was living in a constant state of tension. Or should we say, terror? Escaping
the war gave her something to live for . . . something to fight
for with all her heart. Alone in Australia, Maria had nothing but
her loneliness and pain. Safe in her apartment, Maria was bombarded with the intense grief and loss of her family and her home-
land. Now that the tensions and battles were over, Maria was ready
to die.

In no way can we attempt to minimize the depth of Maria's pain and
suffering, but we can learn something about the important role tension plays
in having a vibrant faith in God. When Maria's tension and struggle ended,
her will to live evaporated.

The same is true for you as a follower of Jesus. If there is never tension
and struggle in your walk with God, your faith loses its muscle. You no longer
totally lean on God. If you've been feeling pounded by the battles you've
been fighting, that's a sign of "holy tension" in your life. To live an intense
life means to live "in tension." And let's face it, being a Christian is intense.
Totally intense.

If your faith is not worth fighting and struggling for, then what do you really
have to live for in this world? Winning the Super Lotto? Will riches really make
you happy? Will free and unlimited sex? An NBA contract? A fifty-million-
dollar Nike endorsement deal on par with Tiger Woods?

All these things we read about, hear about, and see as we channel surf
the television networks are sure enticing and attractive. The only problem is, like most things in life, that these things are too good to be true.
We have a high calling to live not by what is too good to be true but
by truth. If we want to live by the truth, God's truth, we are intentionally choosing to live a life of tension. Never trade God's truth
for the absence of tension in your life. Jesus said it himself,
"In this world you will have trouble, but take courage. I
have overcome the world." Stay on the battlefield.
Be totally intense for Jesus.

(That's all!)

How can I have a Christlike attitude when I'm on the court?

Direct me in the path of your commands, for there I find delight.

PSALM 119:35

Do I need to have an attitude check before I walk on the court?

Examine yourselves to see whether you are in the faith; test yourselves. Do you not realize that Christ Jesus is in you—unless, of course, you fail the test?

2 CORINTHIANS 13:5

How can God's Word help me focus when I compete?

Fix these words of mine in your hearts and minds; tie them as symbols on your hands and bind them on your foreheads.

DEUTERONOMY 11:18

I sometimes have a foul mouth on the court; how can I change this?

Put away perversity from your mouth; keep corrupt talk far from your lips. Let your eyes look straight ahead, fix your gaze directly before you.

PROVERBS 4:24–25

I get really anxious before a match and I have trouble focusing; how can I calm down?

Above all else, guard your heart, for it is the wellspring of life.

PROVERBS 4:23

My thoughts can get really negative when I'm losing; how can I be more positive?

Therefore, holy brothers, who share in the heavenly calling, fix your thoughts on Jesus, the apostle and high priest whom we confess.

HEBREWS 3:1

Concentrating on Christ

*I have trouble concentrating during my races because I get so
distracted; how can God help me concentrate?*

Let us fix our eyes on Jesus, the author and perfecter of our
faith, who for the joy set before him endured the cross, scorn-
ing its shame, and sat down at the right hand of the throne
of God.

HEBREWS 12:2

Keeping Your Cool

Unsportsmanlike Conduct

Unsportsmanlike conduct may be a great
show for the spectators, but it doesn't do the
team much good. Or your relationship with God.
People are watching to see if your life as a Christian really means something. On the court, some
Christians make more dents in God's kingdom than actual differences. So how do you stay in control while competing?

Keeping your cool happens before you even get on
the court. It's called getting mentally prepared. It's
also the time to get spiritually prepared. You're not
only going to battle against your physical opponent; you're also up against your spiritual opponent, the devil. The Bible promises that "greater is
he who is in you than he who is in the world." God
will protect you from Satan getting the edge on
your emotions. The Bible says not to give Satan a
foothold. That means don't give him anything to boost
him up because he'll try to trip you up. Spend some
time praying about your match; ask God to give you
his grace to practice his presence on the court and to protect you from saying something you might regret. Tell him you
need his strength to help you focus on him and to help you do
what you need to do for his glory.

Why do I have such a hard time trying to control my temper toward the referee?

For the sinful nature desires what is contrary to the Spirit, and the Spirit what is contrary to the sinful nature. They are in conflict with each other, so that you do not do what you want.

GALATIANS 5:17

There's a lot of gossip on my team; is this harmful?

A perverse man stirs up dissension, and a gossip separates close friends.

PROVERBS 16:28

My friends make fun of me because I try to settle disputes on the team; how should I react?

But even if you should suffer for what is right, you are blessed. "Do not fear what they fear; do not be frightened."

1 PETER 3:14

Where can I turn when my "Christian" team is plagued with bad attitudes?

May the God who gives endurance and encouragement give you a spirit of unity among yourselves as you follow Christ Jesus.

ROMANS 15:5

What can I do to get along better with my teammates?

Bear with each other and forgive whatever grievances you may have against one another. Forgive as the Lord forgave you. And over all these virtues put on love, which binds them all together in perfect unity.

COLOSSIANS 3:13–14

What can I do when my coach and I disagree on practically everything?

Keeping Your Cool

Starting a quarrel is like breaching a dam; so drop the matter before a dispute breaks out.

PROVERBS 17:14

Winning at All Costs

Ego Trips

Cutthroat competition brings out the worst in us. Well, most of us. If you're a highly competitive person and winning is tops on your priority list, you probably live for challenge. Our society holds up winners and blows off losers. Losing isn't very socially acceptable in this day and age. But the "win at all costs" attitude sometimes produces a lot more heartache than it's worth.

For the person who has to win at all costs, whether through tantrums, cheating, or acting like a rabid beast, their tough outside is probably hiding an insecure and scared inside. A poor self-esteem is pretty stiff competition. To beat a poor self-esteem, the person has to first hide it and then try to prove how good he or she really is by winning all the time. At any cost. At that price, winning isn't worth it.

The only person who had a good "win at all costs" attitude is Jesus Christ. He won eternal life by conquering sin and death through his death and resurrection. He wanted to win for you. He won to overcome lousy self-esteems. He won to defeat the steaming pressure you put on yourself to win. He won so you could win eternal life for free. Eternal life is the one thing you don't have to earn. Jesus Christ already won it. It's a victory that costs you nothing. It's a free gift that makes you free.

I keep fighting the urge to win at all costs; can God help me with this temptation?

He holds victory in store for the upright, he is a shield to those whose walk is blameless.

PROVERBS 2:7

How can I make my relationship with God and others more important than winning?

Let love and faithfulness never leave you; bind them around your neck, write them on the tablet of your heart. Then you will win favor and a good name in the sight of God and man.

PROVERBS 3:3–4

My parents put tremendous pressure on me to win; should I try to please them?

Am I now trying to win the approval of men, or of God? Or am I trying to please men? If I were still trying to please men, I would not be a servant of Christ.

GALATIANS 1:10

I know I can't win on my own; will God help me?

You give me your shield of victory, and your right hand sustains me; you stoop down to make me great.

PSALM 18:35

I try to bring attention to myself when I win; how can I remember to give glory to God?

So whether you eat or drink or whatever you do, do it all for the glory of God.

1 CORINTHIANS 10:31

What should I do when my friends tell me that I'm too competitive?

Be completely humble and gentle; be patient, bearing with one another in love.

EPHESIANS 4:2

Can I be a winner for God even when I lose?

But thanks be to God! He gives us the victory through our Lord Jesus Christ.

1 CORINTHIANS 15:57

Winning at All Costs

Future Fears

One of my favorite places to go running is a place called Doheny Beach Road. It's a beautiful stretch of beach with volleyball courts, campgrounds, and barbecue pits. My favorite time to run is at sunset. As I look out at the Pacific Ocean—the long, curving coastline heading south toward San Clemente and Dana Point Harbor to the north—I see one of the most incredible views I've ever seen. Painted by the glowing sunset colors, Beach Road is an easy place to let go of my worries and frustrations about the future.

One evening while I was jogging at Doheny, I noticed a large group of people around a bonfire. Some were standing, talking in groups of three or four. A few people were cooking hamburgers and serving dinner. Others were sitting down listening to someone who had stood up to talk. While all this was going on, I noticed more people driving in to join the group. People were greeting each other with big bear hugs. This didn't look like your average beach party. By the way everyone dressed, it was obvious they came from different economic backgrounds. Some appeared wealthy, others looked poor. Teenagers, middle-agers, and old-agers, this gathering was a definite mixed salad. The laughter, smiles, hugs, and warm atmosphere that poured out of this group would make anyone feel welcome to grab a hamburger, sit down next to the fire, and stay awhile.

I was intrigued and stopped to watch as I sipped some water. I'd never seen a group like this before at the beach. Something about them was different. A spirit of life and enthusiasm permeated the air. For as many obvious differences this group had, positions and prestige didn't seem to matter. They were all different, yet somehow, all the same. *Some shared experience has bonded them,* I thought.

For a few minutes, I couldn't figure out what this group was all about, but then I overheard someone say "A.A." This was an Alcoholics Anonymous meeting. The differences, smiles, and laughter all made sense to me now. The party they were throwing was probably a celebration of their sobriety. A chance to live drug-free, alcohol-free lives. They were on the road to recovery and were ready to live again.

One day at a time. That's the way people in A.A. try to look at life. Wouldn't it be wonderful if we all looked at life like that? The past is gone, and we can't predict the future, so all we have is today. Jesus said to his followers, "So do not worry, saying, 'What shall we eat?' or 'What shall we drink?' or 'What shall we wear?' For the pagans run after all these things, and your heavenly Father knows that you need them. But seek first his kingdom and his righteousness, and all these things will be given to you as well. Therefore do not worry about tomorrow, for tomorrow will worry about itself. Each day has enough trouble of its own" (Matt. 6:31-34).

My mom's got a plaque on her wall that says, "I may not know the Master's plan, but I know he's got one and I'm included." I know a lot of young people who are scared about the future. They wonder, "Does God even have a plan for my life? If he does, am I really included?" This chapter is written to address those fears, worries, and questions that can paralyze us and keep us from being all that God has designed us to be. Maybe no one has ever told you or perhaps you've never realized it, but God does have a plan for your future. He wants you to live one day at a time trusting him. He understands yesterday, today, and tomorrow like no one else, and his plan for your future is perfect.

God also cares for you like no one else. It's so easy to get consumed by the worries and pressures of trying to fit in, attempting to be different, and hoping to make something out of who you'll be someday. If you've been trying too hard to control, worry, or manipulate your future, you can let go. God knows who you are now, who you used to be in the past, and who he's creating you to be. Leave the future to him. He's got it under control. *Live one day at a time.* Do what Jesus says: Don't worry; tomorrow's got enough headaches and struggles of its own. He's not asking you to ignore your problems or pretend they don't exist. He just wants you to lay them at the foot of the cross, so you can experience the freedom and power of his resurrection. Yesterday's party is over, and tomorrow's party may never get here. Celebrate life today knowing that the Master has a plan, and you're included.

Living by Faith
In the Dark

If you've been a Christian for a while now, you've probably heard someone say, "How could you be so blind to put your trust in something or someone you can't even see? Who'd want to live by blind faith?" Maybe you're not a Christian yet and you've asked yourself the same question, "Am I crazy to trust in this thing or concept called God?" Well, faith and blindness are two different things, but a lot of people want to lump 'em together like camels and humps, dogs and tails, bananas and peels. Blindness is inability to see. Darkness. Pitch black. The Bible simply says that faith is believing in the things we can't see. Everyday, you believe in things you can't see. Important stuff like air, sound, microwaves, and radio waves. Next time you're eating a TV dinner (microwave and heat rays) watching your favorite TV show via satellite with the volume blaring (radio waves) as you inhale and exhale (oxygen), ask yourself, "Am I living by faith? Am I crazy or blind to believe in something that's helping me to exist at this very moment?" Can you live without faith that air exists? No way. Can you live without believing in the Creator of air and the very One who created your lungs to be filled with something you can't see? Hmmm . . . *is that blind faith?*

What is faith exactly?

> Now faith is being sure of what we hope for and certain of what we do not see.
>
> HEBREWS 11:1

Will God give me more faith if I ask?

The apostles said to the Lord, "Increase our faith!" He replied, "If you have faith as small as a mustard seed, you can say to this mulberry tree, 'Be uprooted and planted in the sea,' and it will obey you."

LUKE 17:5–6

I want to do great things for God, but how can I be sure my life will amount to something?

"I tell you the truth, anyone who has faith in me will do what I have been doing. He will do even greater things than these, because I am going to the Father."

JOHN 14:12

My friend says that faith, only faith, is what heals a person. Isn't it Jesus who does the healing? I'm confused.

By faith in the name of Jesus, this man whom you see and know was made strong. It is Jesus' name and the faith that comes through him that has given this complete healing to him, as you can all see.

ACTS 3:16

Will my faith grow if I read the Bible more?

Consequently, faith comes from hearing the message, and the message is heard through the word of Christ.

ROMANS 10:17

I'm dismayed by how weak my faith really is; can God strengthen me?

For Upper-classmen Only

After all the speeches are made and the yearbooks are signed, life after graduation changes in a way that you never expected. Just last June, you and the rest of the senior class were frothing at the mouth like chained bloodhounds waiting for graduation. Now that fall is here, life looks a lot different.

Some students go right to a four-year college, others go to the local junior college, some to trade school, and still others into the work force. Adjustments come easy to some, but others take a nosedive into depression, stress, and frustration over what to do

(Very good stuff!)

☞

Be on your guard; stand firm in the faith; be men of courage; be strong.

1 CORINTHIANS 16:13

How can I trust God if I can't see him?

We live by faith, not by sight.

2 CORINTHIANS 5:7

Trusting God

Promises, Promises

I promise I won't tell anyone. I promise to meet you at eight o'clock sharp. I promise I'll never date anybody but you. I promise I'll be your best friend forever. Yeah, right! You hear promises made and promises broken all the time. You wonder, "Why don't people just tell the truth and really mean what they say?" *I'll try not to tell anyone, but if what you tell me is really juicy, then I'll probably tell a couple friends. I'm going to be late. You are one of many girls I'd love to date. I'm sick of hanging out with you.* A lot of pain and grief could be avoided if people would say what they mean and mean what they say. But life doesn't work like that. Good intentions—you've heard them all before. Some people really mean well, but they can't seem to get their act together. They'd keep a promise and stick to their commitments if they knew what a real commitment is. Right? Wrong. You're tired of broken promises.

God is sick of broken promises too. He hears them all the time. But you know what? Despite all the broken promises he hears (including a bunch of our own), he continues to love and be faithful to those who can't seem to keep their word. He loves each person on this earth so much that he kept his ultimate promise by sending his Son, Jesus, to bridge the gap that separates us from him. Jesus kept his promise too. Even though he had all sorts of distractions and temptations to pull him away from going to the cross, he persevered and did his Father's will. God's Word is filled with literally thousands of promises (that's what this book is all about!) so you can experience a radical friendship with your heavenly Father. If you've been let down by others and feel like you can't trust anyone, go to God. The One who promises everything you need for this life and the next will never let you down.

Why should I trust God?

God is not a man, that he should lie, nor a son of man, that he should change his mind. Does he speak and then not act? Does he promise and not fulfill?

NUMBERS 23:19

Will God keep all his promises to me?

You know with all your heart and soul that not one of all the good promises the LORD your God gave you has failed. Every promise has been fulfilled; not one has failed.

JOSHUA 23:14

I have let God down, but he never lets me down? Why is God like this?

You have kept your promise because you are righteous.

NEHEMIAH 9:8

How can I develop a greater love for God's promises?

with their lives. I've noticed that high school grads struggle in four major areas. Four areas nobody talks about before you graduate. If nobody's told you about the changes everyone goes through after high school, here's some inside information that will help you when you need it.

Friendships

The friends you had in high school may end up being your friends for life. Or they may not. One thing is for certain: After high school, friendships change. They may change for better or for worse, but they will change. Your best friend may move across the country to go to a university. You may decide you want to become a logger in the Pacific northwest and move away from your friends. Change isn't negative if you understand what the change is and you don't fight against it. A lot of friendships become stronger and tighter because of change. Talk with your

(There's more!!)

I rejoice in your promise like one who finds great spoil.

PSALM 119:162

Will God promise to strengthen my faith if I ask him?

Yet he did not waver through unbelief regarding the promise of God, but was strengthened in his faith and gave glory to God, being fully persuaded that God had power to do what he had promised.

ROMANS 4:20–21

I don't understand; why is God so slow in answering my prayers?

The Lord is not slow in keeping his promise, as some understand slowness.

2 PETER 3:9

Why does God promise us so many things?

Through these he has given us his very great and precious promises, so that through them you may participate in the divine nature and escape the corruption in the world caused by evil desires.

2 PETER 1:4

Regaining Your Confidence

Negative Thoughts

Whoops! You blew it again. You muffed the final shot. You studied all night long and still got a D. You got a great award in a music contest, but your mom said there were a few notes that needed work. Nasty voices run inside your head, killing your confidence by telling you you're no good, you're not enough, you'll never measure up. Confidence killers not only destroy how you feel about yourself and others, they also demolish your relationship with God. You have an enemy named Satan

104　　　　　　　　　*Regaining Your Confidence*

who's got a detailed game plan to destroy your confidence in God. There are all sorts of ways he'll use to whittle away your confidence. The Bible says he's like a roaring lion ready to pounce on and devour you like chopped liver. He doesn't care what you believe as long as you don't believe in God.

If you're feeling timid, weak, insecure, and your confidence is about as high as the curb, remember that God believes in you even when you don't believe in yourself. Having God and his strength can give you the courage to tackle any negative thought, feeling, or insecurity you may have. He believes in you like no else! Check out what God's Word says about real abundant life. God's into building confidence. Confidence in him.

Where can I turn when it seems I'm lacking confidence in just about every area of my life?

For you have been my hope, O Sovereign LORD, my confidence since my youth.

PSALM 71:5

How can I remember that I don't have to fight my battles all alone?

"With him is only the arm of flesh, but with us is the Lord our God to help us and to fight our battles." And the people gained confidence from what Hezekiah the king of Judah said.

2 CHRONICLES 32:8

What will I gain by putting my confidence in God?

friends about what you think life will be like after high school and about what might be different in your friendship. New jobs, moving away, new interests, different classes will affect your time schedules and priorities. That's worth talking about. Change is scary when it catches you off guard. Thank God, the one thing that won't change is his friendship toward you.

Family
Once you graduate from high school, not only does your legal status change, your family status changes too. You're no longer just a kid in high school. Regardless of what your folks say, you are now a contributing member of society. Will the same be said about how you contribute to the quality of life in your family? As soon as the grad night party is over, your parents' expectations may change real quick. You may have to pay rent if you're living at home. You may

(See page 107)

Regaining Your Confidence

The fruit of righteousness will be peace; the effect of righteousness will be quietness and confidence forever.

ISAIAH **32:17**

Do I need to feel timid when approaching God?

In him and through faith in him we may approach God with freedom and confidence.

EPHESIANS **3:12**

Why should I place my confidence in God?

Let us then approach the throne of grace with confidence, so that we may receive mercy and find grace to help us in our time of need.

HEBREWS **4:16**

Do I need God's strength to make me a more confident person?

So we say with confidence, "The Lord is my helper; I will not be afraid. What can man do to me?"

HEBREWS **13:6**

Will God even listen to me?

This is the confidence we have in approaching God: that if we ask anything according to his will, he hears us.

1 JOHN **5:14**

Developing Endurance

Hold On

 Do you ever feel like you don't know what to say? You find out your best friend's mom has cancer. What do you say? Your dad loses his job. What do you say? Your girlfriend's family is wacko. What do you say when people come to you with com-

have to pay for some or all
of college. Taking the family car may
not be as easy as it used to be. Your parents
may be cool during this transition, but whatever
happens, you're no longer in high school. Your role in
your family is even more important as you begin to make your
own decisions as an adult. Something to think about . . .

Finances

From the moment you arrive in your mother's arms as a newborn until
the time you're eighteen, your parents will have invested over a hundred
thousand dollars in cold, hard cash to raise you. That's a lot of dough. If you're
like a lot of graduating seniors, you probably haven't taken any financial seminars lately. It's not too late! Finances can be one huge headache if you haven't
learned how to properly save, spend, and separate your priorities when it comes
to cash flow. Gas, car payments, insurance, rent, food, clothes, spending money,
books, tuition . . . you're going to need a lot more money than you did in high school.
You could avoid a wallet-load of problems by learning how to do a budget, figuring
out how much you're earning, what your expenses are, and what things you'd like to
do in the future that require cash, check, or charge. Banks don't care if you don't know
how to balance your checkbook, but they will take your hard-earned cash for bounc-
ing a check.

Future

What are you going to do after high school? You'll hear that question a million times.
Whether you know for sure that you'll be a brain surgeon or you're still trying to figure out what life will be like without a locker, it's all right not to have it all figured
out. Who knows what you'll be doing five to ten years from now? One person . . .
God. You can breathe a lot easier when you realize that wherever you go, he promises to lead you. He knows and understands the future. All the big decisions and
changes you'll be facing are ones he can handle. He wants to be a part of your
future. Be sure to keep him at the center of your plans, because he's got
great ones especially for you. "For I know the plans I have for you,"
declares the Lord, "plans to prosper you and not to harm you, plans
to give you hope and a future" (Jer. 29:11).

(That's all!)

plex problems that don't have easy answers? How can you possibly help others stay afloat when all you're holding onto is your rubber ducky? Sometimes the best thing to say is nothing at all. Or maybe a simple, "Hang in there." I know it sounds trite and won't solve problems, but it can show others you care. When you tell someone to hang in there, you're giving them the confidence that you believe in them. You're telling them you believe they've got what it takes to make it through their problems.

God's Word is designed to help you hang in there when times are tough because, sometimes, hanging in there is all you can do. The best place to hang is in the arms of God. He's the one who'll support you, give you strength, encouragement, perseverance, courage, and peace. God defies all gravity. He's got what it takes to help you hang. He promises never to leave you or forsake you. Never, ever, ever. Hang in there and hang on tight.

Does God have the power to help me with my struggles?

The Lord knows how to rescue godly men from trials.

2 PETER 2:9

I've cried out to God, but is he really listening?

The righteous cry out, and the LORD hears them; he delivers them from all their troubles.

PSALM 34:17

What should I do when I need help changing my attitude during hard times?

108   *Developing Endurance*

Consider it pure joy, my brothers, whenever you face trials of many kinds, because you know that the testing of your faith develops perseverance.

JAMES 1:2–3

Why is God allowing me to experience problem after problem?

In this you greatly rejoice, though now for a little while you may have had to suffer grief in all kinds of trials. These have come so that your faith—of greater worth than gold, which perishes even though refined by fire—may be proved genuine and may result in praise, glory and honor when Jesus Christ is revealed.

1 PETER 1:6–7

I thought Christians didn't have problems like everyone else . . . am I wrong?

A righteous man may have many troubles, but the Lord delivers him from them all.

PSALM 34:19

How can I help a friend who's going though the same struggle I've had before?

Praise be to the God and Father of our Lord Jesus Christ, the Father of compassion and the God of all comfort, who comforts us in all our troubles, so that we can comfort those in any trouble with the comfort we ourselves have received from God.

2 CORINTHIANS 1:3–4

What is my hope for the future?

For our light and momentary troubles are achieving for us an eternal glory that far outweighs them all.

2 CORINTHIANS 4:17

Is it possible to experience God's peace in every situation?

Now may the Lord of peace himself give you peace at all times and in every way.

2 THESSALONIANS 3:16

Making Decisions

I Can't Decide

You face hundreds of decisions each day. That means hundreds of thousands each year. Possibly gigabillions in a lifetime. The decisions you make today will affect you for the rest of your life. It's crucial to understand that good decisions have a cost. You may become unpopular. You may lose a few friends. People will say your good decisions are bad decisions and their bad decisions are good ones. They'll turn your desire to do good inside out, upside down, and backwards instead of forward. Bad decisions come cheap but in the end cost a lot. Bad decisions can ruin your life. Good ones won't.

God promises to give you wisdom if you just ask him (see James 1). He wants to give you everything you need for counting the cost to follow him. He's seen too many young people suffer from lousy decision making. That doesn't have to be you! When you feel like you can't decide what to do, when you've got to choose between following God and everyone else, take time to think through the consequences of your decision. What will the outcome be? Will your decision hurt or help those you really care about? Does your decision please God or hurt him? Remember: If you follow the flock, you could end up a lamb chop.

Will God give me wisdom to make good decisions?

For the LORD gives wisdom, and from his mouth come knowledge and understanding.

PROVERBS 2:6

Making Decisions

I'm confused; who's really in control when decisions are made—me or God?

The lot is cast into the lap, but its every decision is from the LORD.

PROVERBS 16:33

I've seen so many of my friends suffer from making stupid decisions; how can I show them there's a better way?

Who is wise and understanding among you? Let him show it by his good life, by deeds done in the humility that comes from wisdom.

JAMES 3:13

I wrestle with trying to please God and my friends. Why should I do what God wants instead of what my friends want?

Blessed is the man who finds wisdom, the man who gains understanding, for she is more profitable than silver and yields better returns than gold.

PROVERBS 3:13–14

I've made some bad decisions and suffered the consequences . . . how do I start over?

Wisdom is supreme; therefore get wisdom. Though it cost all you have, get understanding.

PROVERBS 4:7

How can I convince a friend that it's important to make good decisions?

Seek good, not evil, that you may live. Then the LORD God Almighty will be with you, just as you say he is.

AMOS 5:14

Can I always count on God's guidance in making wise decisions?

The LORD will guide you always; he will satisfy your needs in a sun-scorched land and will strengthen your frame. You will be like a well-watered garden, like a spring whose waters never fail.

ISAIAH 58:11

How will making a bad decision affect me?

Do not be deceived: God cannot be mocked. A man reaps what he sows.

GALATIANS 6:7

Depending on God
I Hope This Works

Have you ever tried to fix a busted engine with the wrong set of tools? Or lift a gigantic piece of furniture up a narrow staircase and try to squeeze it through a teeny, tiny door? Young people often think that knowing God is like trying to fix something they know won't work. *If I just try harder, if I just work at it a little bit longer, if I just figure where every-thing fits . . .* Hope like that really isn't hope. It's hit and miss chance. It's trusting in something unreliable and unknowable. The God of the Bible is nothing like that. He is knowable, reliable, trustworthy, lis-tening, caring, compassionate, loving, and interested in your life. When you put your hope in him, you're not trusting in something that may blow up in your face. You're hoping in the One who created hope.

Depending on God

What does it mean to put my hope in God?

Show me your ways, O LORD, teach me your paths; guide me in your truth and teach me, for you are God my Savior, and my hope is in you all day long.

PSALM 25:4–5

How can I be sure God will answer my prayers?

You answer us with awesome deeds of righteousness, O God our Savior, the hope of all the ends of the earth and of the farthest seas.

PSALM 65:5

Getting Back in the Sandbox

Homework. Three tests on Thursday. After-school sports. Part-time job. PSAT exams. "What am I going to do after high school? What am I going to do with my life?" Sound familiar?

I don't know about you, but there are times when my life is hurried, worried, and full of stress. Somehow, I don't think this is how God has designed our clocks to tick. Life in the fast lane doesn't have to be life in the frantic lane, but how can you slow down when there is so much to be done and so little time to do it?

It's time for young people to get back into the sandbox of life to relearn what it's like to have a few hours of good clean fun. Living life on purpose means making "playtime" a regular priority. I don't mean carving time out of our week to be childish or immature, but rather, setting aside consistent, fun-filled times to be childlike. Recreation means to re-create, or in simpler terms, to play: shoot hoops, run with your dog, take a nap, or hang out with friends. A key characteristic of a child of God is the ability to play and enjoy God's creation.

Here are some play-filled thoughts on how to hit the turn signal, pull out of the frantic lane, and enjoy the journey of life in the slow lane.

(See page 115)

☞

Depending on God

What can I do when I'm scared my friends won't trust in God if I blow it?

May those who hope in you not be disgraced because of me, O Lord, the LORD Almighty; may those who seek you not be put to shame because of me, O God of Israel.

PSALM 69:6

What should I say when my friends tell me I'm crazy for putting my hope and trust in God?

Blessed is he whose help is the God of Jacob, whose hope is in the LORD his God.

PSALM 146:5

Will God disappoint me like others do?

And hope does not disappoint us, because God has poured out his love into our hearts by the Holy Spirit, whom he has given us.

ROMANS 5:5

Is hope in God something that's really alive and worth giving my life to?

Praise be to the God and Father of our Lord Jesus Christ! In his great mercy he has given us new birth into a living hope through the resurrection of Jesus Christ from the dead.

1 PETER 1:3

Making Sense out of Life

Black, White, and Gray

 Let's get one thing straight: Most of the time, life doesn't make sense. Some people believe life makes sense all the time: it's black and white; everything has a reason, and there's a concrete

> **Today . . .**
> Fly a kite, run in the sprinklers, tickle a child, tell a joke,
> sleep in, encourage someone, blow a bubble, write a letter,
> eat a cookie, ride a bike, watch a sunset, dream a dream,
> let go of a balloon, give a smile, wipe a tear, light a fire, call home,
> make a sand castle, sing a song, share a secret, destroy a fear,
> love someone who's lonely, play tag, chase a cloud, turn off the TV,
> go for a swim, finger-paint, spread some hope, laugh 'til it hurts,
> catch a fish, forget a worry, read a book, say a prayer, nap under a tree,
> jump rope, build a fort, lay on the couch, go to the zoo, climb a rock,
> leave work early, lift a frown, forgive a failure, challenge a doubt,
> buy a puppy, go out to dinner, brave a defeat, surprise a friend,
> admit you're wrong, throw a snowball, roll in the leaves, plan a
> vacation, buy two scoops instead of one, risk an adventure,
> say "I love you," play, pick a flower, count the stars,
> let go of a hurt, think a new thought, wink for no reason,
> reach out because, invent a new game, go barefoot, walk your cat,
> breathe easy, rejoice in a gift, live as a child, live like you mean it,
> not as you wish it, dance with the Giver,
> live, live on, live today.
>
> (That's all!)

explanation for all problems. That's kind of a monochrome way of looking at life. Other people believe that because life doesn't make sense, it's therefore meaningless and no one should even attempt to make sense out of the insensible. (Dress code for this group is black.) Still others believe that if everyone would just be positive, listen to the earth's vibrations, meditate on the rainbows in their navel, and converge with the lunar tidal pull, the whole world would sing in perfect harmony. This life is difficult, it does get confusing, and there are millions of issues, problems, and gray areas that may never be answered . . . in this life. God who stands both in our time zone and outside of time itself, is interested in helping you make sense out of life. This life and eternal life. His Word may not give you the exact answer on how to solve the problem of environmental waste or explain why both humans and monkeys eat bananas, but it will give you understanding at how to approach life, how to get life, and how to live life in a way that makes sense.

Why do some people say such stupid things?

A man who lacks judgment derides his neighbor, but a man of understanding holds his tongue.

PROVERBS 11:12

How can I follow God more closely?

Let me understand the teaching of your precepts; then I will meditate on your wonders.

PSALM 119:27

Why is there such an abuse of justice in this world?

Evil men do not understand justice, but those who seek the LORD understand it fully.

PROVERBS 28:5

I don't understand; how come no one is interested in following God's ways?

The LORD looks down from heaven on the sons of men to see if there are any who understand, any who seek God. All have turned aside, they have together become corrupt; there is no one who does good, not even one.

PSALM 14:2–3

How is it that others seem to know so much about this life, but I feel clueless?

I am your servant; give me discernment that I may understand your statutes.

PSALM 119:125

Making Sense out of Life

I feel like I don't know where my life is going; how can I know God is leading my life?

A man's steps are directed by the LORD. How then can anyone understand his own way?

PROVERBS 20:24

I'm overwhelmed at how awesome God's creation is; is it even possible to understand it all?

As you do not know the path of the wind, or how the body is formed in a mother's womb, so you cannot understand the work of God, the Maker of all things.

ECCLESIASTES 11:5

My stupid decisions get in the way of living the way God wants me to; what should I do?

Therefore do not be foolish, but understand what the Lord's will is.

EPHESIANS 5:17

How do I know what is right?

I do not understand what I do. For what I want to do I do not do, but what I hate I do.

ROMANS 7:15

Having God's Protection

My Personal Bodyguard

Nobody wants to be known as a wimp or a weakling. Who wants to be the center of scorn, rejection, and ridicule? Who wants to be made fun of? No one. Not even Jesus. But you know what? Jesus Christ was made fun of. He was ridiculed. People thought he was crazy, a complete idiot for saying the things he said. Jesus had no one to protect him. No one to stand by him, help him out, or volunteer to take his place. The only one who even attempted to help was Peter. He made a slave's ear into sushi, but even Peter wouldn't take on the Roman soldiers.

Jesus understands fear. So does his Father. That's why the Bible is filled with verses that talk about protection. God wants to protect you from all sorts of fears: enemies, danger, physical harm, depressing thoughts, the unknown, past sins, ridicule, and humiliation. In a sense, he wants to be your personal body-guard. He's not a personal thug or someone to do your dirty work . . . he's still the God of the universe, but he's interested in your safety. He's given you his Word to assure you that what-ever you go through, he's right by your side.

Is there ever going to be a time when I won't have any enemies?

Deliver me from my enemies, O God; protect me from those who rise up against me.

PSALM 59:1

I'm scared to walk to school alone; will God walk with me?

The LORD will protect him and preserve his life; he will bless him in the land and not surrender him to the desire of his foes.

PSALM 41:2

Am I bothering God when I ask him for help with my problems?

In the day of my trouble I will call to you, for you will answer me.

PSALM 86:7

Can I be confident that God is with me in the midst of trouble?

Though I walk in the midst of trouble, you preserve my life; you stretch out your hand against the anger of my foes, with your right hand you save me.

PSALM 138:7

Having God's Protection

Where is God when I feel like He's hiding from me when I come to Him with a problem? When David was in trouble, did he ever feel like God was hiding from him?

Do not hide your face from your servant; answer me quickly, for I am in trouble. Come near and rescue me; redeem me because of my foes.

PSALM 69:17–18

I'm feeling bombarded with temptation; is God really going to protect me?

But the Lord is faithful, and he will strengthen and protect you from the evil one.

2 THESSALONIANS 3:3

Did Jesus actually pray for his disciples' protection? Is he praying for me?

"I will remain in the world no longer, but they are still in the world, and I am coming to you. Holy Father, protect them by the power of your name—the name you gave me—so that they may be one as we are one."

JOHN 17:11

Overcoming Bad Habits

Nail Biters Anonymous

 I'm a fingernail biter. Most of the time, I do it without thinking, but if you're a nail biter like me, you understand. When I was little, I used to chew my fingernails raw. Then I stopped for a long time, years even, but somehow, a couple years ago I started up again. People who don't have gross habits like me say that nail biters are worrywarts. Nail biters are nervous, anxious, or worried about something in the past, present, or future, so they

try to take their minds off what they're doing by biting their fingernails. That's me. I do worry about things, lots of things. That's why I'm glad I know the God who cares about what's on my heart. I can give him my problems. I can trust him with things I have no control over. I know he wants to replace my worries with peace. And I'm depending on him to give me the strength to stop biting my fingernails. I'm grateful God promises me peace instead of stinging pain.

My nervous habits drive others crazy; will God help me change?

Do not be anxious about anything, but in everything, by prayer and petition, with thanksgiving, present your requests to God.

PHILIPPIANS 4:6

Where is God when I need his Word to soothe my stress-filled life?

When anxiety was great within me, your consolation brought joy to my soul.

PSALM 94:19

I know I can't do anything to change the future, but how can I keep from worrying about it all the time?

"Therefore do not worry about tomorrow, for tomorrow will worry about itself. Each day has enough trouble of its own."

MATTHEW 6:34

I don't spend much time alone with God because I'm worried about so many things; can anyone relate?

Overcoming Bad Habits

"Martha, Martha," the Lord answered, "you are worried and upset about many things, but only one thing is needed. Mary has chosen what is better, and it will not be taken away from her."

LUKE 10:41–42

What would life be like if I trusted God instead of worrying?

"But blessed is the man who trusts in the LORD, whose confidence is in him. He will be like a tree planted by the water that sends out its roots by the stream. It does not fear when heat comes; its leaves are always green. It has no worries in a year of drought and never fails to bear fruit."

JEREMIAH 17:7–8

I'm so stressed about all my problems that I don't see much growth in my walk with God; why is this?

The one who received the seed that fell among the thorns is the man who hears the word, but the worries of this life and the deceitfulness of wealth choke it, making it unfruitful.

MATTHEW 13:22

How can I give God my worries and frustrations?

Search me, O God, and know my heart; test me and know my anxious thoughts. See if there is any offensive way in me, and lead me in the way everlasting.

PSALM 139:23–24

Tackling Problems

Overcomers Anonymous

There's a group at my church called "Overcomers." The people who come to Overcomers have, in one way or another, been beat up by life. Drugs. Sexual abuse. Alcohol. Unhealthy relationships. Addictions. Lousy family relationships. Whatever kind of problem or tragedy you can think of, these people have faced it. That's why they're in Overcomers. Hitting their problems head-on, admitting they're powerless over their lives, and depending on God to help them make healthy decisions are just a few ways they're rearranging their lives.

Are you an overcomer? If you've realized you can't handle life on your own and you need the help of an almighty, awesome, and ever-loving Father, then you're in the process of overcoming. Jesus Christ came to this world to overcome sin, death, tears, pain, and suffering. In him, you can be an overcomer. Who has ever overcome your life with love like that? His Word promises to give you strength when you're weary, power when you're weak, and hope when you feel life is hopeless. When I'm feeling beat up and discouraged from my problems, this Bible verse reminds me, regardless of how I'm feeling, that I'm an overcomer in Christ. "He said to me: 'It is done. I am the Alpha and the Omega, the Beginning and the End. To him who is thirsty I will give to drink without cost from the spring of the water of life. He who overcomes will inherit all this, and I will be his God and he will be my son'" (Rev. 21:6–7).

I have so many enemies; what am I supposed to do?

My enemy will say, "I have overcome him," and my foes will rejoice when I fall. But I trust in your unfailing love; my heart rejoices in your salvation.

PSALM 13:4

Can I count on God to help me in every situation?

The cords of death entangled me, the anguish of the grave came upon me; I was overcome by trouble and sorrow. Then I called on the name of the LORD: "O LORD, save me!" The LORD is gracious and righteous; our God is full of compassion.

PSALM 116:3–5

Tackling Problems

I'm afraid of getting beat up at school; what can I do?

"They will fight against you but will not overcome you, for I am with you and will rescue you," declares the LORD.

JEREMIAH 1:19

I'm trying really hard to live as God wants me to, but all I run into is trouble; how can I keep from being discouraged?

"I have told you these things, so that in me you may have peace. In this world you will have trouble. But take heart! I have overcome the world."

JOHN 16:33

How can I overcome my fear of failure?

"For I am the LORD, your God, who takes hold of your right hand and says to you, Do not fear; I will help you."

ISAIAH 41:13

I feel like I'm under constant attack from Satan; what should I do?

You, dear children, are from God and have overcome them, because the one who is in you is greater than the one who is in the world.

1 JOHN 4:4

Will Jesus help me overcome my problems?

They will make war against the Lamb, but the Lamb will overcome them because he is Lord of lords and King of kings—and with him will be his called, chosen and faithful followers.

REVELATION 17:14

Journal Entry

_____

_____

_____

_____

_____

_____

_____

_____

_____

_____

_____

_____

_____

_____

_____

_____

So What Difference Does Faith Make?

_____

_____

_____

_____

_____

_____

_____

_____

_____

_____

_____

_____

_____

_____

_____

_____

_____

_____

_____

_____

_____

_____

So What Difference Does Faith Make?

So What Difference Does Faith Make?

_____

_____

_____

_____

_____

_____

_____

_____

_____

_____

_____

_____

_____

_____

_____

_____

_____

_____

_____

_____

_____

So What Difference Does Faith Make?

So What Difference Does Faith Make?